KEEPING THE LIGHT
IN YOUR EYES

A guide to helping teachers
discover, remember, relive,
and rediscover
the joy of teaching

"Teaching is the kindling of the flame."
Socrates

Beth Hurst
SOUTHWEST MISSOURI STATE UNIVERSITY

Ginny Reding
PLEASANT HOPE MIDDLE SCHOOL

Holcomb Hathaway, Publishers
SCOTTSDALE, ARIZONA 85250

Dedication

To my boys—Kevin, Joe, and John.
BH

To Kenny, Royce Michael, and Joshua Paul with love and gratitude.
GR

Library of Congress Cataloging-in-Publication Data

Hurst, Beth.
 Keeping the light in your eyes : a guide to helping teachers
discover, remember, relive, and rediscover the joy of teaching /
Beth Hurst, Ginny Reding.
  p.   cm.
 Includes bibliographical references and index.
 ISBN 1-890871-05-2
 1. Teachers. 2. Teachers—Attitudes. 3. Teaching. I. Reding,
Ginny. II. Title.
 LB1775.H89 1999   98-22224
 371.1—dc21   CIP

Holcomb Hathaway, Publishers
6207 North Cattle Track Road
Scottsdale, Arizona 85250

10 9 8 7 6 5 4 3 2

ISBN 1-890871-05-2

Printed in the United States of America.

Contents

Preface

This book is my catharsis. When I came home from my very first day of teaching, I ran in the door, hugged my husband, and thanked him for encouraging me to go back to school to get my teaching degree. I told him that I would be at that school for the next 30 years. Four years later, I came home from school, fell into my husband's arms in tears and cried, "I quit." What brought me to this point so quickly in my career? How do I keep it from happening again? I'll answer the first question here; the rest of the book answers the latter.

The year I started teaching, our state came out with a new achievement test. Teachers were given a list of objectives for each of the subject areas and told to teach those objectives. When I looked at the objectives and then looked at my textbooks, I found at a glance that the two did not mesh. I went to my principal and said, "As a new teacher, I don't know if I am supposed to teach what is in the textbooks, or if I am supposed to teach the objectives given to us by the state."

He answered, "We need to teach what the state requires us to teach."

That's all I needed to know. I set out to learn what it was I was supposed to teach. Much of the material, especially in science, was new to me. I remember spending an entire day with my dad, who was also a teacher, while he went through the list of objectives and taught me what I was not able to find easily elsewhere.

Each of the four years I taught, I continued to learn with my students, and found teaching to be one of the most rewarding experiences of my life. My students were performing quite well on the tests because we were learning together. I studied those objectives and strove to teach the concepts to the best of my ability. I loved my students, and I loved learning.

Then one Friday afternoon my principal walked to my door and said he needed to speak with me. He left the secretary with my students and took me to the conference room. There was an ominous feeling in the air. He sat me down and told me that another teacher had accused me of cheating on the state test. One of my students who had an Individual Education Plan (IEP) was required to have someone read the test to her. The teacher who had read her the test felt the student "knew too much and knew the answers too quickly" for someone with a learning disability. Later that day, I reminded the principal that the student had been tested and found not only to have a reading disability, but also an IQ of over 145. Of course she knew the material; we had studied it extensively.

But at that time, I was a new, untenured teacher who was afraid. I did not sound as confident as I might now. He kept me at school that night until 6:00 P.M., long after everyone else had gone home. He told me he would speak to the superintendent, call a school board meeting if necessary, and I would be fired on the spot if they decided I had cheated. Needless to say, I was absolutely devastated. I was scared. I was hurt to the depths of my soul. And I spent a weekend in hell.

The following Monday, I waited all morning for the arrival of the principal to my room. As I was standing outside at noon recess, I saw him walking around the building laughing and joking with the children. He walked past me smiling and said a casual hello. I timidly asked him if there was something he wanted to tell me. He responded by saying, "Oh, that. I went home and talked to my wife, who is a teacher. She said 'That's every teacher's fear; they are told to teach those objectives and then when they do, they are accused of cheating.'" He then said, "I didn't give it any more thought after that."

Two weeks later I turned in my resignation. That same principal was quite surprised when I told him I was quitting. He said he couldn't understand why good teachers like me quit teaching. I never told him why. Actually, this incident was the last of several frustrations; it was just the straw that broke the teacher's back.

Upon entering graduate school to begin work on my master's degree, many doors began to open up to me. Wonderful opportunities presented themselves. Life was good. I had the chance to teach preservice teachers on the college level. I fell in love with teaching all over again. I had quickly forgotten how incredibly fulfilling it is to teach. But I was scared, and I was scarred. What if it happens again? What if I let myself get completely lost in the joy of teaching again and someone tries to pull it all out from under me once more?

Well, I am stronger this time, and I am determined. I am determined that no one will ever take from me what I am not willing to give. The joy that I receive from teaching is so tremendous that I now protect it like I do my own children. No one can take that away from me again. It is my light. I will not hide it under a bushel out of fear that someone can blow it out. There is an old saying: "The same wind that blows out a candle also fans a fire." Today I let my soul blow in the wind, fully confident that it will take me higher and higher to grander and grander places. And today I have my students to go to those places with me. What good company they are. I am truly blessed to be a teacher.

Beth Hurst, Ph.D.

Acknowledgments

We would like to express our deepest thanks to the following people: Colette Kelly, our editor at Holcomb Hathaway, for her support, encouragement, and advice; the many teachers who so willingly shared of themselves as we prodded with questions and deadlines; and our parents and family members who enthusiastically showered us with warm wishes and wise words.

Sincere thanks, too, to the following individuals, who reviewed this book and offered suggestions for its improvement: Claudia Cornett, Wittenburg University; Tanya Henderson, Mt. Vernon High School; Kathleen S. Jongsma, Northside ISD; Ronda Beaman, Northern Arizona University.

Introduction

We were on a mission. We set out to find teachers who, even after years in the classroom, still find teaching an enjoyable and fulfilling career. In a profession in which pressure, stress, and little thanks come with the territory, it is easy for teachers to get discouraged, burned out, and want to quit.

Much research has been dedicated to the subject of teacher burnout. The May 1997 issue of *Time* magazine reported the following: "One survey found that 40% of public school teachers would not go into teaching if they had to choose a career again. According to the federal Department of Education, 30% of new teachers leave the classroom within the first three years. Those who stay feel overworked, underpaid, underappreciated—and poorly prepared."

In their national study, Heath-Camp and Camp (1990) found three sources of burnout for beginning teachers: "(1) system-related problems such as inadequate orientation, equipment, and supplies; (2) such student-related problems as lack of motivation and undesirable behavior; and (3) personal struggles with self-confidence, time management, and organizational skills." From a study of elementary, intermediate, and secondary teachers, Byrne (1992) reported that findings were "consistent across groups in revealing the potency of role conflict, work overload, classroom climate, decision-making, and peer support as the primary organizational determinants of teachers burnout." Hollingsworth (1990) identifies two sources of teacher burnout as "(1) work overload, excessive paperwork, and repetitive tasks; and (2) isolation from other teachers which leads to loneliness."

The list goes on. It seems simple to identify causes of burnout, more difficult to find a cure. In writing this book, we have drawn heavily from the experiences of real teachers who, having faced the problems all teachers face, get up each morning ready and eager to enter their classrooms. We searched for these teachers' secrets of success in hopes of finding an answer.

As we talked with dozens of teachers around the country, we found a theme in their answers to the question, "What keeps the light in your eyes?" Teachers may talk for hours about what they do and how they feel, but in the final analysis, what keeps the light in their eyes can be boiled down to three things.

First, teachers themselves love to learn and find that the more they learn, the more they want to learn. Knowledge is in itself a reward. Second, they have learned to bring their own likes and interests into their teaching. They look for ways to make learning meaningful not only to their students but to themselves as well. And last, and as they will tell you, most important, they love their students. As they see their students succeed and see the light of understanding in their eyes, they know their work is worthwhile. They are proud to stand among the ranks of those who change lives. They know they have made a difference.

This book includes many real-life experiences of teachers. Quotes, anecdotes, and stories are interwoven with practical suggestions for putting new ideas into practice. The book, following the theme of "Keeping the Light in

Your Eyes," is divided into four parts. The intent of Part One, "The Source of the Light," is to guide you as you reflect upon your original passion for teaching. "Kindle the Flame," Part Two, offers ways to reclaim your enthusiasm when you feel it is waning. We hope Part Three, "Keep the Light Shining," will provide you with the impetus for continued learning and growth. And finally, Part Four, "Bask in the Glow" speaks to the joys we experience when we take the time to stop and contemplate our accomplishments as teachers.

While many books have been written with an emphasis on improving the education of students, few books deal specifically with the affective aspects of teaching. Our goal is to help you as a teacher sustain or renew your original enthusiasm for teaching. Although our objective is to support teachers, we believe that a secondary benefit will be that students are also positively affected. In an age when it is becoming increasingly difficult to stimulate our students, we believe that one way to do so is for us as teachers to be enthused.

If you are a beginning teacher, seek from this book help in learning how to deal with the emotional demands of teaching. Learn how other teachers remain happy and inspired after years in the classroom. To veteran teachers, especially those who are feeling some burnout, we hope you will be motivated by new ideas and new paradigms to change the way you view yourselves and your roles in your classrooms. To university students who are in training to teach, we hope you will find the book useful as you search for ideas about how to fulfill your dreams of becoming the kinds of teachers you want to be. And finally, to retired teachers, we hope this book fills you with wonderful memories of the years you dedicated to improving our world.

As you read this book, it is our hope that you see yourself in the stories told by your fellow teachers. Be encouraged and inspired by the knowledge that your efforts equip others to live life more fully and more successfully.

PART ONE

THE SOURCE OF THE LIGHT

WHERE DOES IT BEGIN?

Most of us begin our teaching experience full of vim, vigor, and vitality. Excited and enthusiastic about this new adventure, (and naive regarding educational politics), we make plans to change the world, one classroom at a time. We create bulletin boards, hang posters, stamp textbooks, arrange learning centers. Out with the old, in with the new. We plan, design, create, organize, and dream about our first day. And when it arrives, we stand at the door, beaming, welcoming our students into their "home away from home" for the year.

The pressures and demands of teaching can, more quickly than we'd like to think, begin to rob us of that original passion and enthusiasm. The light that once gleamed in our eyes as we dreamed of our first classroom can be dimmed by the reality of the stresses of our job. When that light begins to dim, one way to revive our passion is to recall our reasons for becoming teachers.

Remember that time when you just knew that you knew. You knew that you would make a difference. You knew that you would be a part of something very special. You knew that you would be a teacher.

Defining the Light

Light guides the way; it directs. A light shines in teachers' eyes as they talk about what they do and for whom they do it.

Perhaps the number-one reason most of us become teachers is because we want to make a difference in students' lives. We remain in the profession because of the difference our students make in our lives. The glow of that "light of understanding" when they finally grasp something we have been trying to teach gives us fulfillment. We teachers have a "light of understanding" as well. Why is it hard to define that light? Because the light is different things for different people. It is whatever keeps us going; whatever motivates us as teachers. Some of us are driven by strong emotion, passionate desire; some are motivated by the gratification of inner needs; still others feel the need to serve. It may be the evidence of the pride and the joy we feel as we see our students succeed. Whatever your motivation, whatever the light is for you, keep it before you.

From prospective teachers to retired teachers, there is an energy—the light—that keeps finding its way into our eyes when we talk about learning and kids. I (Beth) remember sitting in my education classes, my eyes filling with tears every time I even heard the word "teacher." I couldn't wait to be a teacher. I never really understood why I would get misty-eyed until years later when I was sharing my thoughts about the joys of teaching with a college class of prospective teachers. One student, Michelle Thomason, wrote an essay about the light that came in her eyes as she thought of becoming a teacher. I was moved by how her words seemed to express what I had felt when teaching was still a dream for me. I have kept her essay all these years. It is important that I remember what that light is for me.

"In my mind I see a classroom. Desks are arranged in communities surrounded by bright bulletin boards and learning stations. Individual students' projects are scattered about. I can hear laughter and the 'a-ha's' of learning, but there are no faces. There are no children in the desks. There is no teacher.

The image is clear, yet misty. Perhaps the mist is the tear in my eye that always comes when I think of this room. It is not a tear of sorrow. Oh, no! It is a tear that holds all my emotional being—all my hopes and dreams. It is the same tear that comes to my eyes when I hear the national anthem or think of my family. It is a tear of pride.

I am very proud of my decision to become a teacher. I know I will have great responsibilities and challenges, but I will also have tremendous rewards. These rewards are not monetary, and may not come in the form of gratitude. The greatest rewards will be the memories of my future students. I know one day a student will think back and say, 'That teacher really made a difference in my life.'"

I also know that one day my room will be filled with desks arranged in communities surrounded by bright bulletin boards and learning stations. There will be laughter. There will be faces. Students will fill the desks and look to the teacher for guidance, and that teacher will be me."

Not all of us have those kinds of emotions when we think about becoming a teacher. To me (Ginny), choosing teaching as a career seemed natural. I was calm about it. Didn't feel much passion. I just knew that's what I was going to do. But I still had a light. I still had a dream. I knew what I wanted, and I felt a responsibility to do it well. Such differences among teachers help make learning an exciting, unique experience for our students. The students are under the wings of a variety of people from a variety of places with a variety of dreams.

Genny Cramer has been teaching for many years and is director of a university graduate reading program, but she only recently came to a surprising insight.

"I didn't realize until about three years ago why I became a teacher and stayed a teacher. I thought it was because I had a calling to teach, which is probably partially true. I also thought I had specialized in reading because it was such an important barrier to subject-area learning, which is also probably true. But it came as a sudden blinding shock to me to realize that I became a reading teacher to help better understand the traumatic beginning I had as a child when I was learning to read. I was so miserable and afraid as a second-grade nonreader.

When I was five, our family moved from a city where I had attended a parochial kindergarten for about six months of school to a one-room school district about 30 miles away. I was allowed by a kind teacher to be in 'kindergarten' by myself for the remaining two months of the eight-month school year, scribbling, drawing, and playing, with the plan that I would start first grade the next fall. With a new teacher the next school year (actually several in rapid succession), I was put into second grade since it was evidently assumed I had been in the first grade the previous year. For some reason—perhaps pride or shyness—neither I nor my parents nor any classmates let the teacher know I really should be starting first grade. I found myself a second-grade student who could neither read nor write nor do simple math—looking in confusion, bewilderment, and failure at second-grade reading, math, spelling, and other materials which were incomprehensible to me. I stared down at the squiggles and marks on pages and knew there had to be a system to all this, but I wasn't getting it. It was a miserable year. I was overwhelmed and couldn't seem to learn anything.

The next year our one-room school consolidated, and we were bussed into town school for third grade. There another student and I had special assignments. When everyone else had 20 spelling words, we had 10. When everyone else had 30 math problems, we had 15. I was firmly certain that I was stupid and had trouble learning. Even today, my first thought when beginning difficult reading, writing, or math tasks is to say to myself, 'You are so stupid. You can't learn anything. You will never be able to learn anything.' It takes effort even now to work through these feelings, and the best way for me always is to begin enjoying what I am doing.

I finally began to read when my sister and I sat down and she read fun and easy books to me. I listened and took in the stories, and as we repeated them, I began to read small parts. I had to feel safe, to feel unjudged, to have some fun, and to grasp some meaning before I was able to begin to read successfully.

Now I try to set up class situations in which students feel safe, are not judged, have fun, and learn. When I need to teach second- to twelfth-grade content-area reading for example, I use strategies like Radio Reading to set up the conditions of security, acceptance, enjoyment, and education. In Radio Reading, students are placed in groups of three to five and given a reading passage at their independent or instructional levels. Students pretend they are radio announcers reading for the radio. Some teachers like to make tin-foil microphones or use actual microphones and tape the students reading aloud. Students are encouraged to rehearse the material as an announcer would and to ask for help on words they don't know. Students write questions over the segments they are going to read aloud and after reading, ask a question to each member in their group as in a radio interview. We talk about ten-inch voices (where only those ten inches away can hear) and put students knee to knee as they read the segments they were assigned. When one student is reading his or her segment, the other students keep the passage turned over so they can't read along. This teaches the students to listen carefully. All my students have great fun with this reading activity, as do I.

In the middle of the fun, however, important learning is taking place. The students are practicing fluent reading, not using the traditional round-robin pattern. They strengthen listening as they attend to the person reading aloud. They help their questioning, usually at inferential and even evaluative levels as well as literal levels, as they shape the questions they ask the other members of their group. They also learn important content-area information through the selection of the passage or text section used. All of this, and the students and I are laughing and bouncing as we learn.

I discovered Radio Reading when reading Vacca and Vacca's third edition of *Content Area Reading* (Scott, Foresman, 1989). The current edition includes many other similar strategies to make reading meaningful such as Stauffer's Directed Reading-Thinking Activity, which leads the reader with prediction strategies, and Manzo's ReQuest, in which students ask the teacher questions.

Students like myself—frightened, overwhelmed, and confused—benefit so much from this kind of fun in the classroom. However, school instructional time is quite important. I have to feel I know what I am doing in the classroom and why I am doing it, and so do my students. Our classroom time is too precious to spend on fun without goals of learning in mind. That same time is also too precious to ignore fun when it ignites learning. Robert Sylwester, who has studied much of the recent information on brain research, suggests that we ignore emotion to our peril in the classroom. Emotion, such as having fun, draws attention, which draws the brain to learning. It was certainly true of myself as a six-year-old when I began to have success in reading and learning.

In my own life, this scared little girl now loves to learn, read, and write. I seek to find ways to pull other frightened or disinterested students, whether children or adults, into the joy, movement, and energy found in learning. The only way I have found to do it is to be excited about learning myself."

Fuel for the Fire
IDEAS TO INCORPORATE

- Reflect back. Take a moment to let go of the worries of piles of paperwork, grades to figure, files to sort. Instead, think of the beginnings of your dream. Why *are* you here? Somewhere inside you, that dream is still alive. You can make it vivid again. Write yourself a note about why you became a teacher, seal it in an envelope, and write on the front: "Open in case of emergency." On a day when thoughts of quitting dampen your spirit, open the envelope.
- What is the "light" for you? It is important for each of us to define what motivates us to teach. Write one sentence defining what the light is for you. Tape it to your desk as a reminder, or type it on the computer using a special font and graphics and frame it to put on your desk.
- We were surprised that so many teachers seemed grateful that we asked them to talk or write about what they do to keep teaching "alive" for them. As one teacher said, "Whether you use what I said or not, I'm glad I did this. It made me stop and think about how glad I am to be a teacher. Sometimes I forget." Stop and take a moment to write down your reasons for being a teacher. What keeps the light in your eyes?
- Write about events from your childhood that either influenced you to become a teacher or influenced the kind of teacher you are today.

Just for the Preservice Teacher

- Michelle Thomason wrote about her dreams of becoming a teacher. Take a few minutes to write down what images come to mind when you close your eyes and think about your future classroom.

What Brought You Here?

There is a reason you are in the classroom. What is it?

Although we recognize our differences as teachers, we also celebrate the fact that we are alike in many ways. When asked "What brought you to the teaching profession?" it is interesting that teachers' responses fall into groups of similar categories. Our colleagues in classrooms are teachers who are there because they love the kids, they feel called to a mission, or are motivated by their students' success.

It's the Kids

When prospective educators are asked why they want to become teachers, they often respond by saying, "I just love kids." There is much more to being a good teacher than enjoying kids, but that love is still in the heart of a good teacher. You can love kids and not love teaching, but you can't love teaching and not love kids. Fulfilled teachers love their subject, and they love their students.

A love for students is at the center of a teacher's heart.

Fourth-grade teacher Lori Elliott shares her response to a student who wonders why she teaches.

"Not long ago our class went on a field trip and one of my students' parents followed us in their car. When it came time to head back to school, Kelly's parents asked him if he would like to ride back with them instead of on the bus. He answered, 'No, I want to sit in the front and talk to Mrs. Elliott.'

We rode awhile and he finally turned to me and said, 'Mrs. Elliott, I want to ask you a question I've been wanting to ask you for a long time.' And then he said, 'Why do you teach?' I guess I looked at him funny because he then said, 'Do you just like the things we do or do you like the kids?'

I told Kelly, 'I love the kids. I couldn't do the kinds of things we do if I didn't love you.' Kelly sat up tall with a broad smile covering his face, and said, 'I knew it! I told my mom you love the kids best of all. That's why you teach!'

Then Kelly turned around in his seat with a smug look on his face. It amazed me that he had been waiting all year to ask me that question. Later, when we got back to school, he ran to his mom and said, 'I told you so!'

His mom said, 'Yeah, you're right. She'd have to love you guys to do all the things she does for you.' That's why I do what I do. I tell my kids I love them because I do love them."

Tanya Henderson, high school English teacher, agrees it's the kids that keep her going.

"There are days I don't like my job. Sometimes I have too many papers to grade, or I'm hurriedly calculating semester grades for the following morning, or the administration is pushing me to go to a workshop I really don't have time to attend.

But when I'm down, I remember to stop and enjoy the kids. I teach high school kids who, on the surface, seem to be more concerned about getting driver's licenses and keeping their jobs than learning. Even though they're bigger, have acne, and are a little more moody, I know that underneath their tough, 'mature' exteriors, they still want to please their teachers. They like seeing their teachers smile, getting a pat on the back, reading positive comments on papers they've written, and they like to learn something new and interesting.

> "We find delight in the beauty and happiness of children that makes the heart too big for the body."
>
> Ralph Waldo Emerson

Funny, the whole time I'm trying to make them feel good and enjoy school, I notice that I start to feel good and enjoy school more too. When I make an effort to be patient and kind, even on my most stressful days, all my troubles melt away, and I start to really love my job again. The kids really make a difference to me."

When elementary teacher Kate Companik was asked what keeps the light in her eyes after 23 years in the classroom, she quickly responded,

"Oh, that's easy; it's the kids. Each morning I see them running down the hall in a hurry to our classroom, and every day I have to tell them to walk. Then I know why I am here. It is their enthusiasm for learning that keeps me enthused. Recently, I was explaining to the kids a new project we would be working on. We were going to make papier-maché peaches to show the sequence of events in the literature set we were reading, *James and the Giant Peach*. They got so excited they would barely let me finish telling them about it. They were ready to go. This makes what I do fun for me because it is so much fun to them. For me, teaching is like a cycle—I choose things to do that I know I will enjoy, and the kids enjoy it so much that it makes me enjoy it even more.

As an example, I enjoyed *The Indian and the Cupboard* when I read it, so I chose it for the class to read as one of our literature set units. We did activities which pertained to the book such as make a cupboard of a scene from the book, study the Iroquois Indians, and make False Face Society Masks. We tried to build a longhouse, but after some difficulty, decided Native Americans must have been very clever. We moved on to another project. After we finished the book, we watched the

> "Each morning when I see my kids running down the hall in a hurry to our classroom, I know why I am here."
>
> Kate Companik, teacher

movie and had a literary discussion comparing the book to the movie. As usual, they liked the book much more. It is fun to see my kids get so much enjoyment from a book.

Even if I am doing a project I have done before, it is still exciting for me because of the excitement of the kids. I love the way they make me laugh. I can be down in the dumps and they will cheer me up. If you don't have a good time teaching, maybe you're in the wrong profession."

Cindie Hendrix, high school English teacher, says she loves teenagers—in her classroom and in her family. "Those teenage years are the most fun," she says.

"Why do I teach? I just love it. I love my subject. I love to read. I prefer upper secondary students because I consider myself a bridge. Many important people have helped my students come to this bridge—teachers, parents, mentors—but I have the privilege of helping them cross it. They are crossing over to adult life, and I want to help them make the transition as smoothly as possible. Grammar, writing, and vocabulary prepare them to be efficient in the world of college and work; however, literature teaches them about life. I want them to step over into this new life prepared.

I love to see how far I can get students to go without driving them or myself crazy. I love the challenge. Last year was the greatest challenge. I was new to my school system and was told there was a gap from the junior high level to where I had the kids in eleventh grade. I started with the basics. We worked hard, and we got where we needed to be. It was a big rush—a challenge. I loved it because I knew I had so much to do to get them where they needed to be."

Tracey Hankins, recently nominated for Teacher of the Year in her school district, says that students are at the heart of her love for teaching.

"These kids become such an important part of my life. They are the reason I get up every day to go to work and face the many challenges we teachers face. As I reflect back on my years of teaching, I feel as though my students are like my own children. It is so hard to turn loose of them to let them go on to the next grade level.

Kids can say things in passing that you'll cherish and never forget. One year I wore a sweatshirt to school with the logo MSTA, Missouri State Teachers' Association, on it and one of my students, Diana Kaercher, asked me what MSTA stood for. Being the experienced teacher I was, I turned her question around and asked her, 'What do you think it stands for?' Diana replied, 'Most Special Teacher Alive!' I had just received the compliment of my life. Another teacher in our district heard the story and shared it with the state MSTA office. The next year, MSTA used 'Most Special Teacher Alive' on all of their promotional items. What an honor that was for me.

"The truth is that I am enslaved . . . in one vast love affair with seventy children."
Sylvia Ashton-Warner

Just as Diana made an impact on my life that day with just a simple comment, I realize that I am making an impact on each and every child's life in my classroom by the way I act and the things I say. And just as her comment had a larger impact on other teachers across our state, I never know what larger impact my words will have. It is my goal to touch as many children as I can. The little compliments we give each other really do make a difference!

It is wonderful to be able to go to work knowing that I will receive smiles and hugs from children all day long. Some days do not seem bright; as a matter of fact, sometimes it feels as though I have hit rock bottom, but then I face a small child who lets me know that he or she needs me to be there in full force, and it helps me put things into perspective. I pray often that I continue to enjoy teaching throughout my career. I want to keep the flame burning."

It's a Mission

Teaching is one of those jobs. You've read the bumper stickers or mugs: "If you can't do, teach." Seems like we get a lot of bad press. The world is falling apart; blame the schools. Want a job with little to do and three months' vacation? Teach. But we're teachers; we know the truth. And if the truth be known, when there is no one in the lives of some children— there is a teacher. There is always a teacher. When the chips are down, teachers plug along. When conditions are bad, when risks are high, tough teachers stick it out. When the media steps on our toes, we dig in our heels and try harder.

Teaching the children is a calling for some; if it is yours, you can't do anything but.

The school where I (Ginny) work has a career education program that teaches students about a variety of careers. At the same time, they can evaluate themselves for jobs that match their own abilities and interests. It is always interesting to see students' choices. I am on the junior high level, so naturally these young people are still doing a lot of dreaming and anticipating. But many of them take this task very seriously and diligently research their job choices.

When they try to match their abilities and interests on the career search, they find the teaching profession under "helping" occupations. Teachers are givers. Obviously, there are some in our ranks who give us black eyes. But overall, teachers come from a melting pot of people with something in common. They are optimistic about the future generation, and they are a caring group. That's why, for many teachers, their job is a mission. It's a calling. They are where they are because that's the only place they can be.

After years of teaching in an elementary classroom, at the age of 59, Hazel Rathel became a student once again and earned her specialist degree. She became the principal of an elementary school, a state department consultant, and a part-time supervisor of student teachers at a local university. Now retired, she says she found an excitement and joy in the career to which she was drawn. She encourages teachers to continue to learn, to use every method possible to reach students and to take available courses and workshops. Hazel tells the story of what led her to the classroom.

"As I look back over my life, I see the way of teaching being pointed to me. I grew up on an orange grove at the edge of town near Orlando, Florida. There were ten of us children in the family, and I was the oldest of the younger and the youngest of the older children. My three oldest sisters were unable to complete high school because we were a very poor family and transportation was not available. These three had the keenest minds and never stopped learning or teaching. They regularly checked out books from the library and kept us all involved in reading.

I had a brother and three sisters younger than I, and I felt that I must prepare them for first grade. My brother told me that he didn't have to learn anything in first grade because I had already taught it to him. I discovered early to use all sorts of tricks to get a child to learn. We played games and used lots of drama. I made up plays which we performed for our parents and older sisters. I realize now that I later carried this into my classroom as I used many creative ways to teach. I started teaching as a six-year-old child, partly because my older sisters had taught me.

"Every action of our lives touches on some chord that will vibrate in eternity."
E. H. Chapin

I found my mission in teaching, and after all these years, I still get excited about it. I would love to do it all over again."

High school science teacher Cathy Carleton doesn't have to think long about her choice of teaching as a profession.

"I'm certain I would choose teaching time and again, if given the opportunity. Teaching is what I was put on earth to do. I've known that ever since my decision to begin college. One time, after a particularly grueling year because of school politics, I quit teaching and worked for a neurosurgeon. In a few years I had Ian (my son) and decided to stay home with him. That doctor offered me a profit-sharing plan that would guarantee me half a million dollars by retirement if I would return to work for him when I was ready to reenter the workforce. I gave it a lot of thought and eventually turned him down because I knew when I was ready to work again, it would have to be teaching; I'm just not happy doing anything else."

Tracey Hankins changed school districts, moving from kindergarten level, which she loved, to fifth grade, and later third grade. She felt that it was all a part of a design.

"I guess God has a plan for each of us. I know He put me in that classroom for a reason. That year I had two girls who each had a parent suffering in the last stages of cancer. One of the girls wrote to me two years later, after her father had died, and told me I was not only her teacher, but her friend and a support system for her. This makes me feel that I am making a difference in children's lives. Two summers later, I sadly lost two of my students from that same fifth-grade class. One young man died due to carbon monoxide poisoning in his home, and the other died in a car-bicycle accident. This all happened within three

"Teach as though you were teaching your own children."
Anonymous

weeks. It was such a tragedy! I felt as though I had lost two of my own children. I organized a group support session for any classmates who wanted to come. We told stories about our relationships with the boys and celebrated the time we had with them.

My most recent calling is to teach third-grade at-risk students. I love my job! I have a group of 20 students, 15 of whom are considered at-risk kids. Five students, who have a strong social and academic background and are considered by the school the 'smart kids,' are placed in the class to serve as role models. This makes a wonderful mix. It is exciting for me to see kids who begin the year as at-risk kids and end up the year as role-model kids."

Middle school science teacher Justine Lines also sees teaching as her mission. She wants to help make the world a better place for future generations.

"Every fall before a new school year begins, I try to remember why I chose to teach. My mind goes back to my college days when I was headstrong and thought I knew everything. I was involved in peace and justice issues as well as environmental concerns. My energy was strong and my desire to act as a catalyst for change increased with every headline I read.

I was studying biology and was fascinated with the wonders of the natural world. The future also interested me. I wondered if we would learn to live on the earth to create a sustainable life for many more generations or if we would dig a hole so deep we would never get out. In biology, you could become an active part of the solution by cleaning up creeks, monitoring water, and working with public policy to actually help make the world a better place.

It was during this time that I began to think about teaching as a career. What better way to influence the environment than to teach the next generation of public-policy makers, scientists, and conscientious citizens about the importance of preserving our planet?

As a teacher, I get a great amount of personal satisfaction from teaching kids about the natural wonders of our world. I feel like I am doing something to help change the world one person at a time. When the school politics get rough, as they often do, I go back to the origin of my mission—to make a difference in the lives of kids, thereby helping to make the world a better place for all of us."

Energized by the Success of Your Students

There is an old saying, "Nothing succeeds like success." Nowhere is that idea more true than in the classroom. Success snowballs. One student happens on to a little success, and all the others want to jump on the bandwagon. Good teachers take advantage of that. They plant seeds, water, feed, and nurture, and one day success blossoms.

A paradox exists in this effort: when a teacher stays focused on the success of his students, suddenly that teacher is feeling a taste of victory himself.

Watching your students succeed is motivation for beginning the cycle of teaching again.

When apathy begins to take root, or when the reality of student achievement seems hopeless, tune in to the successes of your students. Provide an atmosphere where success is the only thing that can grow well. Not only will your students blossom but you will be energized by their success.

Veronica Mays knows about this. She began to see tremendous success in her students when she shared with them some principles of learning she had gleaned from her own search for truth. As a child, she struggled in school, and she was determined to find out why. After reading every book she could get her hands on about learning, her passion became to share her newfound knowledge with others who had also struggled.

"As a reading and study skills instructor, I discovered that many students had negative attitudes toward learning. It was all over their faces that they didn't want to be there. They were shut down. As I showed them how everyone can learn, and as I began to explain the different learning styles, especially about right-brain and left-brain learners, I could see the light come on in their eyes. Many of the students had experienced a lot of failure in school. They had been labeled, or had labeled themselves, as 'dumb,' or 'broken,' or 'different,' or they had been told they 'couldn't do anything right.' When I helped them see they could learn and taught them how, they became excited about learning for the first time in their lives.

"My greatest satisfaction comes when my students find the success they never thought they could have."
Addie Rhodes Lee

For example, when my right-brain-dominant students learn that our traditional schools are set up for dominant left-brain learners, they realize they have been mislabeled. They see how the schools value and teach left-brain academic skills, especially math and language, which are based on symbols. Left-brained people like logic, sequencing, analyzing, following directions, and the abstract. Because those skills do not come naturally for right-brain learners, they are often labeled as lazy or told they're not trying. Right-brain-dominant students are more kinesthetic, hands-on, visual learners. They want to see it and feel it—to do something with the information. Listening is the least effective way for them to learn. They need to be actively involved.

To help them learn how to apply their newfound knowledge about learning styles and brain dominance, I have them do activities in class that are designed to meet their needs. For example, since some students need to talk about what they are learning in order to better process information, I have group work where they find information together. For other learners, I use a process called Sketch to Stretch where students draw pictures to help them remember a concept or word. I teach how graphic organizers help right-brain learners 'see' the information from a different angle. For example, if they are studying the branches of the government, they list the three branches across the top of the page and then, under each heading, list the characteristics of that branch. The idea is just to get the words on the page in some sort of image in their mind. Mnemonic devices, which help with memorization, also work well. The important thing I try to do is teach multisensory or whole-brain learning skills. I don't want students to make excuses for why they can't learn. I try to teach them that we can all be like Michelangelo, who mastered both sides of the brain. As students learn these concepts and begin to experience success in learning and school for the first time in their lives, they have a skip in their step. They get fired up, and I can't explain the energy that gives me."

Karen Stanley is the high school business department in her school. She has single-handedly led students to business competitions on the national level seven times, and has taken 216 entries to state contests. What is her secret? Students say that she focuses on their success. Jerrell, a senior, says, "She is tough, but loving. She'll push you to the limits and stretch you. She expects the best out of people." Eleventh grader Jody adds, "She really cares whether you learn. She's tough, but only because she wants the best for you. She is there all the way, saying, 'You're good at what you do. I have faith in you.'" Karen herself is hesitant to put her finger on the success that surrounds her in the classroom. She does admit, however, that she focuses on her students and their abilities to succeed.

"I never intended to be a teacher. When people asked what I wanted to do, I said, 'I don't know, but it's not going to be teaching.' When I found myself in the classroom student teaching, though, something happened. It's that 'watching them succeed' thing. There is a joy in watching students gain skills they can use throughout their lives.

Students learn a great deal in preparing for and participating in competition, not only academically but socially as well. I get a sense of satisfaction in seeing students' confidence rise when they realize, maybe for the first time, they are really good at something.

From January until late spring, I get to school at 7:00 A.M. to meet with students for contest practice. It is hard work and takes initiative on the students' part. The reputation of the program motivates students to want to participate. They've seen other kids succeed in past years, and they want to be part of it. I make my expectations in preparing for competitions very clear. Students must want to participate. They must do their best and commit to follow through, however far their talents take them. My biggest challenge is working with students who have the potential but don't have the desire to develop it. It's hard to get them to realize they can do it if they apply themselves. When they succeed, I feel that I have succeeded.

Probably the highlight of my teaching career was the time I heard that three of my students had placed at the national competition. I was dumbstruck. I knew all three had prepared themselves to the best of their ability. I knew they had a chance to place—but it's so hard to place on the national level. When the awards were announced, it was the strangest thing. I just kept hearing their names called, one at a time. I would think, 'Could _____ be next?' It was all in slow motion, and then I would hear the name. 'That's my kid!' It was unbelievably exciting.

Focusing on my students' success absolutely keeps me motivated. Seeing one group succeed is what makes me want to go back and work with another group to try to do the same."

One thing that stands out about middle school math teacher Cheryl Stroud is her concern that she teach her students in a way that is meaningful to them and that will help them succeed. Maybe that is why she was a finalist for Teacher of the Year in 1997. She spends time looking for authentic examples of what she is trying to teach. For example, she recently used the blueprints for a new cafeteria in her school to work with her students on geometry concepts. She had her students take the measurements from the actual blueprint and scale them down to a proportion of $1^1/_4" = 2'$ on graph paper. After scaling the room on paper, she had the students cut out furniture and arrange it as they thought it would best fit in the new cafeteria. She selected what she considered to be the top six products. She gave them to the students who set up the tables in the cafeteria. They were to try each plan for one week and then select the student's plan that worked best. Cheryl reported that Rocky, the winner, felt a great deal of success as he saw his work on proportions put into actual use.

Why teach? Cheryl says that she goes the extra mile because she wants to show students in her middle school math classes that she cares about them and their futures. She says that some days teaching reminds her of the Peace Corps slogan, "It's the hardest job you'll ever love."

"I try to find ways to get the best from each of my students. I am the only motivator some children have, and I continually look for ways to show students that they are important. I have students tell me what they like to do, what they think of math and school, and what they'd like to be someday. I refer to this information when planning lessons so that I can try to relate their special likes and abilities to the topic I'm teaching. For example, if they mention auto mechanics or veterinary science, I have them explain what they know about how math is used in those areas. This year I was asked by our local newspaper to participate in a weekly sports game where different people predict who will win the upcoming football games and what the statistics will be. I flipped through my cards to find kids who showed a particular interest in football, and selected as the participating class the one I thought would be most motivated by this project. We asked our football 'experts' for their advice on who would win and what the statistics would be, and we looked at the percentages. I brought in as many math concepts as I could while we were working through this. We sent our predictions to the newspaper for publication, and at the end of the football season, the winner closest to the actual outcome was announced. It's a good way for kids to see a relationship between math and their interests.

It's not always easy to find the energy, but it is very important to make time for the student who needs an extra nudge or positive word to keep going. It is a good teacher who loves each student and wants the best for him or her."

"My heart is singing for joy this morning. A miracle has happened! The light of understanding has shone upon my little pupil's mind, and behold, all things are changed."
Annie Sullivan

As a high school librarian, Gwen Jeffries has the opportunity to see students from a different viewpoint than many of us who are in the classroom.

She also is motivated by the success of her students, but perhaps with a little different slant than we often take.

"My favorite part of teaching is seeing young people wake up to the fact that they themselves are their own best teacher. A focused, energetic teenager pursuing an interest of his own in a library is a wonder to behold. It is not a sight one sees every day. I have decided that IQ is not important. Curiosity is. Some people of high IQ have very little curiosity. They may earn high grades by doing what they are assigned. The children with little self-discipline or those who don't memorize well may still succeed in later life when they are allowed to follow their interests. Neither is likely to fly. But the child who combines the willingness to submit to the discipline of a classroom, yet still has in the bottom of his soul an unquenched flame of curiosity . . . this child will fly."

Michael Bell has been teaching graduate students for many years. He still defines the light as the excitement of seeing students learn, and seeing them succeed in a subject they never thought they could. His primary teaching responsibility is to instruct teachers in the process of conducting research in their classrooms. He knows that most of his students enter his room with negative attitudes and preconceived ideas about research, but that doesn't bother him; in fact, he sees it as a challenge.

"Many teachers who take my classes enter the room scared to death of research. Just the word 'research' makes them shake in their boots. I start out by helping them see that no one knows more about what is going on in their classrooms than they do. It is important for them to realize how much they know, how much they can do, and that they are the experts. Once I've convinced them of this, then I can teach them the fundamentals of research and show them different ways to conduct research in their classrooms.

There is only one thing that makes teaching worthwhile—that makes it fun so you want to keep doing it. It is fun to see somebody learn something for the first time. No matter how many years I teach, that's what keeps me going. To hear students say, 'I understand! I got it! I can do it!' makes it all worthwhile. If you don't experience that, you don't have any fun teaching."

Fuel for the Fire
IDEAS TO INCORPORATE

- Write your students a "Dear Class" letter and tell them why you enjoy being their teacher. Provide specific reasons for why you like them as a class. Follow this with a writing activity in which students also write a "Dear Class" letter expressing what they like about the class. Allow students to read their letters to the class, make class books that include the class letters, or extend it into a research activity where they compare the letters and chart the similarities in the responses.

- Buy a cheap camera that you can keep at school and let kids occasionally take pictures of classroom activities. Designate a bulletin board to start a class collage. Invite parents to help with the collage by having a roll of film developed from time to time.

- Keep a copy of your class list handy on your desk. Set a goal to say at least one positive thing to each of your students that week. Put a check by the student's name so you can make sure you have reached each student each week. While this obviously benefits the children, it will bring you satisfaction as well.

- What is your mission? Make a list of the things that are important to you. Then compare your list to what you do in your classroom. Are you doing what you set out to do? If so, give yourself a pat on the back. If not, ask yourself what you can do to fulfill your mission.

- Find a way that fits with your own personality and time schedule to track the successes of your students. Don't become overwhelmed by trying to keep records of every area, but identify something each student does during a particular period of time where he or she has seen some success.

- Go public with success! Recognize the achievements of your students. Display work, post charts acknowledging mastery, send home notes of pride, identify students in daily announcements. Find a way in your own school to achieve this, but keep it simple enough that you don't become stressed trying to keep up.

- Encourage (or even require) your students to set goals for themselves in certain areas. Have them follow their own progress. Hold an occasional class discussion time when students are allowed to share their progress with the group. Make a big deal out of it when someone meets his or her goal.

- Make a list of at least five things in your teaching career of which you are most proud. It might help you to know how often you achieve these things. Recognize what feeds your soul.

- Make a decision about what you are willing and able to give—and then be satisfied with it. Realize that for your students to succeed, there will be a cost to you. They will need to be guided, worked with, and encouraged. It will take effort on your part, but you will gain as much as your students.

Just for the Preservice Teacher

- Make a list of the reasons you chose to become a teacher. Talk to another teacher about why you want to be a teacher.

- What, specifically, do you enjoy about working with children or young people? Write it down and share it with someone.

- Make a list of your school successes. At what kinds of things in school do you excel? Write down some ways you can cultivate the same kinds of experiences for your future students.

What Influenced You?

Remembering early incidents that triggered your desires to teach will bring back memories you shouldn't forget.

Do you remember when you first saw the "light turn on" in someone's eyes—that first glint of understanding? It probably sparked something in you that made you know that you were a teacher. Or maybe from the time you were a child, you played school with dolls, neighborhood kids, or anyone who happened along and would humor you. Perhaps when you were a student, a special instructor sparked your interest in joining the teaching profession. You may have been raised in a family of teachers, and it just seemed to be bred into you that you were one of them. Whatever your situation, something or someone influenced your decision to become an educator.

A Teacher Who Made the Difference

We can all probably think of a teacher in our past who made a big impression on us. For me (Ginny) it was Mr. Sawyers. He was my hero. He was big and strong and knew everything. Mr. Sawyers was my sixth-grade teacher. I remember wandering around the house on a Saturday afternoon thinking that Monday would never come. Oh, how I wanted to be at school. Sounds weird, doesn't it?

You were my teacher; you were my friend. You changed my life.

I don't really know why Mr. Sawyers was so special to me. Maybe it was the fact that he had a nickname for me. He called me Schochie, telling me it meant "little one." That fit me to a tee. I liked being given a special name, but that wasn't the only reason I couldn't wait for Monday. Mr. Sawyers took time to talk with us students, almost as if we were adults. He talked about his son, world issues, his life in the service. He let us into his heart, and I liked that.

I had a very good friend named Kathy. She was as tall as I was short, and Mr. Sawyers teased us a lot. I think he called us Mutt and Jeff, or some such thing. One time Kathy and I were doing a special report on a South American country. When we discovered that coffee beans were one of the country's main products, we decided to make coffee from fresh coffee beans as a part of our project. This was before the days when "everyone" had a coffee grinder. We mashed the beans the best we could, put them in a cup, filled the cup with hot tap water, and proudly presented the "coffee" to Mr. Sawyers. It is my recollection that he drank it. Surely he took one very small sip and poured the rest down the sink. Surely. But at the time, I remember thinking that he felt it was quite good-tasting, and that we were very industrious to have come up with such a brilliant plan.

Mr. Sawyers took time with me, showed an interest in me, and filled a void in my life. I'm sure a big reason he was so special to me was that he was somewhat of a father figure. My father had died several years before. Sometimes teachers have roles they don't even know they have. Whatever the reason, memories of my sixth-grade year have remained in my heart.

Elementary teacher Dianne Renkoski tells about a teacher who significantly influenced her life by taking the time to get to know who she was and what she needed.

"I remember being scared to death of Mrs. Johnson, my high school business teacher, the first time I met her. My junior year I enrolled in her seventh-hour office machines class. It was her first year in the district so I guess she thought she would be extra firm on that first day of school. She was a tall woman with short, flaming-red hair. I can still see her walking around the classroom lecturing us about the do's and don'ts of her discipline policy. When the bell rang on that first day, my best friend and I vowed we would drop her class the next morning. For some reason we stayed.

Her bark turned out to be worse than her bite. Beneath her rough-and-tough exterior, Mrs. Johnson cared deeply about her students. She saw us as individuals with specific needs, and her goal was to help us meet those needs. Whether she was aware of it or not, Mrs. Johnson taught much more than just academics.

"Teachers who have plugged away at their jobs for twenty, thirty, and forty years are heroes. I suspect they know in their hearts they've done a good thing, too, and are more satisfied with themselves than most people are. Most of us end up with no more than five or six people who remember us. Teachers have thousands of people who remember them for the rest of their lives."
Andrew A. Rooney

The first valuable lesson she taught me occurred during a timed typing test. I am a perfectionist, so these tests were extremely stressful for me. On one particular day, Mrs. Johnson set the timer and began walking around the room as usual. I was typing furiously and trying desperately not to make a mistake. My intense concentration was interrupted by Mrs. Johnson randomly pressing keys on my typewriter as she walked by. I stopped instantly and sat like a statue at my desk while the timer kept ticking. What was she doing? How dare she mess me up? When I looked at her in shocked disbelief, she grinned an ornery grin and kept walking. Mrs. Johnson knew me well enough to know I needed to learn that mistakes will be made, but it's not the end of the world.

During my senior year, I enrolled in Mrs. Johnson's two-hour clerical practice class. Her philosophy was that regardless of a student's future occupation, clerical skills would always be beneficial. The curriculum included a mock corporation during the last quarter of the year.

The room was arranged in specific departments such as purchasing, accounts receivable, and accounts payable. We each wrote our top three choices of employment and then Mrs. Johnson assigned us to our specific jobs. She chose me to be the office manager even though that was not one of the jobs I had listed. In spite of my insecurities, Mrs. Johnson recognized my leadership abilities and decided it was time for me to also recognize them.

At the end-of-the-year awards ceremony, Mrs. Johnson presented me with a certificate for being the 'Most Valuable Employee' in our mock corporation.

She said, 'This is a special award voted on by the students in Clerical Practice. This year the vote was unanimous, and I agree with their choice wholeheartedly.' Then she turned to me with tears in her eyes and said, 'You did it, kid!'

Mrs. Johnson made a difference in my life. She showed me that I could do more than I once thought possible. She gently forced me to reach beyond the boundaries I had set for myself. She believed in me and taught me to believe in myself. What greater lesson could a teacher pass on to a student? I have a plaque given to me by a former student that reads, 'To teach is to touch a life forever. Thank you for touching my life, Mrs. J.!' "

Veronica Mays says it was a teacher who turned her life around and taught her to believe in herself.

"Many years ago, I was one of those students who couldn't make it in school. Because of some unfortunate things going on in my life, I was failing sixth grade. I thought I was too stupid to learn. My mom took me to a private school where I met Mr. Grundman, who thought I was ready for seventh grade. He believed in me. Because he believed in me, I began to believe in myself. That was a turning point for me. I began to see some success for the first time. Because of that, I realize how important it is to believe in your students. I will never allow a student to tell me that they are 'dumb' or 'stupid' or that they can't learn."

Preservice teacher Stan Ponder's decision to become a teacher was based on the positive influence of one of his high school teachers, who made learning come alive.

"I never wanted to be a teacher; in fact when I was in high school, I believe I had an underlying motive to make teachers regret their career decisions. That was until Mr. Whelan's eleventh-grade history class. Until then, history to me was boring books and old news that made no difference in my life.

However, Mr. Whelan made history fun, relevant to my life, and most of all, he made it real. I have countless memories of an animated Mr. Whelan waving his arms about, running from one side of the room to the other, trying to give us a mental picture of the subject he was teaching. He acted out parts from history. His lectures were full of life, energy, and excitement. He talked with such passion that even the most uninterested student sat on the edge of his seat. Mr. Whelan even took us out on the football field as an ancient Roman army to show us what a phalanx formation was. From ancient Egypt to World War II, Mr. Whelan knew it all. After his class, I did too. That, in itself, is a miracle. He related history to my life.

"I will act as if what I do makes a difference."
William James

Mr. Whelan wanted us to view learning as an enjoyable experience. He refused to call worksheets 'worksheets.' He called them 'knowledge sheets.'

His theory was that learning should be a fun activity through which one gains knowledge. He felt learning loses its purpose if students view it as work.

Mr. Whelan changed my life. I went from a kid with no direction or future to a young adult with a game plan and a strong future. It is that kind of teacher I hope I can be someday. If I can influence just one child the way Mr. Whelan influenced me, I will be happy with my choice to be a teacher."

It's All in the Family

Those of us who were raised in a family of teachers may feel as though we have grown up with a knowledge of how teachers think, act, and feel. We have had an inside perspective of the workings of schools, classrooms, and teachers' minds. Growing up in a family of teachers is something that we (Beth and Ginny) can talk about from firsthand experience. We are cousins and spent our early years listening to "teacher talk" around the table at family get-togethers. Our grandma sparked an interest in teaching in her own children, and that interest has been passed on. We have parents, aunts, uncles, and cousins who have all chosen to join the teaching profession. So in our family, the stories, lively discussions, aggravations, and accolades most often centered around teaching and school.

When teachers raise you, you are raised to teach.

Grandma died when we were very young. She taught school on Friday and died on Monday. Ginny's memories are vague, and Beth's are only the ones passed down through our family's tradition of storytelling. But we know that becoming a teacher was very important to our grandma.

Because the high school building was in a town far from her home, Grandma had to quit school after completing her elementary years of education. It was the early 1900s, and she had no way to travel the distance. During that time period, sixth graders who were capable and interested were asked to teach the younger children. Grandma was one of those students. She rode a horse to her job. After marrying Grandpa, she quit teaching to raise her family.

"Called people possess an unwavering sense of purpose."
Gordon MacDonald

When her children were in high school, Grandma earned her own high school diploma, and she later graduated from junior college, returning to teaching once again. Teaching school during the winter months, she worked on her bachelor in education degree in the summers. At the age of 45, she graduated from college.

Grandma dearly loved her schoolchildren, and they cherished her. She took their burdens home with her. She would take biscuits to school in the mornings because she knew many students came hungry. I (Ginny) remember one time when Grandma brought a little girl home to stay with her after the girl's house had burned. Grandma had her children and their problems tucked away inside her heart.

When it came time for my (Beth's) mother to start college, Grandpa sold a horse to pay for her tuition. She went to the same college where Grandma had received her teaching degree and where I eventually graduated. All three generations earned lifetime teaching certificates from the same university where I now teach. As I stand in front of my students, I am in the same classrooms, in the same building where my mother and her mother learned how to teach. I feel that I am standing on sacred ground.

The family into which we were born has given us a valuable heritage. We have learned to value life, to love learning, and to want to contribute to the world. That's why we became teachers, and we are grateful for that legacy.

Ruth Skelton, retired after 25 years of teaching elementary students in Missouri and Texas, did not begin college until she was married and her own two children were in school. She had heard a lot of "teacher talk" as she was growing up, and her desire was to be a teacher.

"My dad's family were all teachers. Dad wanted me to do something different, but I really respected all of my aunts and uncles and wanted to be like them. I learned that you can't change the world, but I started out believing that all children can learn, and after 25 years of teaching, I left feeling the same way."

Angie Bixler tells how her mother influenced her to become a speech teacher.

"It was a Wednesday evening, and I went to church with my family as usual. I was downstairs talking with some friends before youth group started when I heard some yelling accompanied by quite a commotion. Then a single raised voice shouted, 'Someone get Louanna,' my mom, who had taught third grade for 29 years. A sixth-grade girl with a behavior problem who had recently begun coming to our church was disrupting children's services, using profanity with the kids and adults, and was fighting with whomever tried to speak to her.

A teacher affects eternity; no one can tell where his influence stops."   Henry Adams

The minute my mom got there, she took the girl calmly by the hand and led her outside. They were gone about 20 minutes, and when they came back the girl was smiling and laughing with my mom, and she sat through the entire church service with her. What did my mother do that made such a difference? She spoke to her kindly, but firmly, and she took the time to show her she cared.

The girl returned the following few weeks and always found my mom to be her seat partner. It was then that all of the late nights of creating bulletin boards, cutting out letters, and passing up of movies to grade science tests began making sense to me. I watched incident after incident like this one, where my mom unintentionally portrayed her unselfish love for and talent with children. I've read Christmas cards, seen thank-you notes, and met people face to face that all speak of the impact my mom made on their lives. What an incredible statement.

It soon became my goal to become one who can put a smile on a troubled child's face and to touch someone's life even if it's just enough so that they remember me when it's Christmas card time. My mom is a walking testimony of everything that epitomizes what a teacher should be. Her life is what inspired me to study speech-language pathology and to make a difference in the lives of others."

That's When I Knew

Life's way of teaching is through experience. What we live, we learn. Our reactions to events that occur in our lives teach us about ourselves; what we learn guides us in making life decisions. Some teachers have memories from childhood of their first teaching experiences. Others realize that people surrounding them recognized their natural teaching abilities long before they themselves did. We may not remember the exact moment in time when we knew we were teachers, but most of us come to a place at some point when we recognize that we are teachers, heart and soul. Ayers (1990) contends that teachers often feel that teaching is not merely what one does, but who one is.

Whatever the circumstances, there was a time when you just knew that you knew.

Retired teacher Mary Wright has felt like a teacher all her life. She found her niche with junior high students, primarily teaching math and English. She reminisces about her early recognition that teaching was something she wanted to do.

"When I was ten years old, my brothers, sister, and I transferred from a big school to a very small one with two grades in one room. My teacher asked me to take some of the students, one at a time, into a large, lighted cloakroom to help them with their reading. I enjoyed helping them read with expression. It was my favorite time of the day, and I was pleased when any of my pupils improved their reading skills, but I was happiest when I saw that they actually understood that the words were telling a story.

Then, when I was 16, I taught four- and five-year-olds in Vacation Bible School. The night of the program a 'very busy' child was to quote his memory verse, 'It is I; be not afraid.' The congregation roared with laughter as he said, 'It's just me; don't be skeered,' but I rejoiced at that small, busy child's ability to put the verse into his own words. I believed then that I could be a teacher.

My teaching opportunities continued through high school as I was able to 'rescue' a fellow classmate who found himself floundering in Spanish and others who came to me for help. Toward the end of WWII, my brother and some close friends, all boys, had been asked to prepare for early admission to the air force. They needed more than average knowledge of math. Since I always enjoyed math and took every math class our school offered, I readily agreed to work with them on their math skills. Night after night, those boys and I sat at our dining room table working together so they could have confidence in their ability to pass the math part of the test. I witnessed a rare occasion when air force officers came to our house soon after my brother took the test and swore him into the air force. Again, I realized that I was meant to be a teacher."

Judy Campbell, a special-education teacher in an elementary school, reflects back on her early desires to teach.

"After tenth grade, I participated in a volunteer service project through my church. The project was in Nebraska at the state hospital. I was assigned to work with three or four retarded children. My time there was unstructured. I mainly was supposed to spend time with them. It touched me; it pulled at my heartstrings to see abandoned children at the hospital.

I knew then that special education was the field I wanted to get into. My father was a teacher, so teaching was a positive thing in my eyes. I certainly haven't regretted it. If I had it to do over again, I would still be a teacher."

Vera Ker is a special education teacher of middle school and high school students. Her journey to becoming a teacher took several detours, but she remembers well her longing to teach.

"I first had the idea of becoming a teacher some time during my middle school years. Then as I reached senior high, I thought I might need to do something else because all my teachers complained every payday about their salaries being so low. My parents lived on a farm. I had always heard them complain about not having much money, so I thought I'd better do something other than teach school if the pay was so low.

At that time we didn't have counselors to give us guidance; my folks had separated, and my teachers talked about how difficult college was. So without encouragement and money, I chose not to go to college in the fall. I got married instead. Marriage took me overseas, where I helped teach Bible classes with a college graduate who had a teaching certificate. Every time she had to spell a difficult word, she looked to me for the correct spelling. I knew I wanted to become a teacher. I thought, if she can graduate from college and teach, so can I. I needed that degree for my own self-esteem. That motivation returned with me to the States, where I immediately enrolled in college for the fall semester. Never again did I consider the salary a detriment to my ultimate goal of becoming a public school teacher."

Fuel for the Fire
IDEAS TO INCORPORATE

- Write a thank-you note to a teacher who made a difference in your life. It will make you feel good that you took the time to say thank you. Encourage him or her to write back by asking for advice in a particular area.

- Invite one of your former teachers to come visit your class and talk to your students. When he or she comes, tell your students stories about when you were a student.

- Have your students write a letter to a favorite teacher they have had. You will be helping them learn how to express appreciation to others.

- How many teachers are in your family? Make a teaching family tree. If there are teachers, can you find where the teaching profession began in your family?

- Ask the teachers in your family to tell you one sentence about what they like best about teaching. Type these on a page with a border or graphics and make copies for each person.

- Think of the time when you knew you wanted to be a teacher. Where were you? What was going on in your life at the time? Make a time line of your life including important events that led you into teaching.

- Bring pictures back to your mind by browsing through personal journals, looking at old yearbooks or class pictures, or reading notes you have received from students throughout the years. Buy a small hand-held-size picture album and make an autobiographical book of your progression to teaching. Begin with a picture or memento of yourself as a child playing school. Include items such as graduation pictures or your first note from a student.

- Do an activity with your students in which you discuss careers. Talk to them about how and when you knew you were going to be a teacher. Help them understand the process of choosing a career.

- Write your own story of your first memories of your desire to teach.

Just for the Preservice Teacher

- Interview a couple of your education professors and ask them why they became teachers. Look for similarities in their reasons for teaching and your own.

- Are there any educators in your family? If so, ask them why they became teachers. Share your dreams to teach with them.

PART TWO

KINDLE THE FLAME

CHANGE YOURSELF AND THE WORLD AROUND YOU CHANGES

"Try to change the world, and the world will destroy you; change yourself, and the world around you changes." This saying has profound educational implications because we leave college determined to solve the problems in today's schools. We begin our first year of teaching bursting with ideas for making things better. What we often discover is that people either do not want to be changed or do not see a need for change; there may even be those who put roadblocks in our paths and dampen our spirits. Discouraged, we may feel that our dreams of making a difference in the world are lost.

Veteran teachers may face the same discouragement. We become weary of "keeping on keeping on," or maybe we have worked hard and seen few results. We might ask ourselves what difference we are making in this merry-go-round of educational ups and downs. We may feel that we must abandon our dreams.

But a change in the way we view ourselves and our roles may be what we need to bring back our passion to make a difference. Instead of trying to change the system, we can change ourselves, thereby changing the world inside our classrooms and our circle of friends and colleagues. While it is true that teachers can and will make a difference, difference begins in our own classrooms, with our own students, and in our own lives. We can begin by looking within ourselves and making changes. In his book *How to Win Friends and Influence People*, Dale Carnegie said, "Perfect yourself first." As we change ourselves, we will be amazed at how the world around us changes.

Change Your Perspective by Changing Your Paradigm

In today's business and educational circles, the term paradigm has come to be defined as a specific way of seeing something. It can also be likened to tunnel vision because we can see only what is directly in front of our eyes; one way is viewed to the exclusion of all else. Joel Barker illustrated this point beautifully in his video *The Business of Paradigms*. One of Barker's examples concerned Swiss watches. Years ago, when one thought of watchmakers, the Swiss immediately came to mind. They were the leading watch makers of the world. When quartz movement was invented, it completely changed how watches are made. Almost overnight the Swiss went from being number one to having almost no market share for watches. Who do you suppose invented the

We can change our world by changing the way we view it.

quartz movement? The Swiss. But when the Swiss inventors took their idea to their superiors, they were told that it wouldn't work. It was too different. The superiors were so sure it wouldn't work that they didn't even protect the idea. The inventors took their idea to a world watch congress, and Texas Instruments and Seiko of Japan walked by, saw the idea, and latched onto it. These two companies now control the worldwide market share for watches. Barker explained that we have to be willing to look beyond what we know to see what is new. That's often as hard for us to do in teaching as it is in other areas of our lives.

It's difficult to change the way we view students and teaching because we have been in school all of our lives. Some of us have always been in school. Sometimes we may want to change the way we teach or our attitudes about teaching, but we just don't know how. One place to start is by changing our paradigms—our one way of looking at teaching—and we can transform our teaching, our attitudes, and ourselves. We begin by asking the question, "How can I see this differently?" and being open to new ideas and willing to take risks.

Trying to change how I (Beth) view and react to students is one way I work on changing my paradigms at school. In my classes for preservice teachers, I require the students to write "Dear Beth" letters. I learned this idea from one of my graduate school professors, Genny Cramer. Genny learned about it at a conference presentation by Jane Hansen at the University of New Hampshire. (Isn't this how teaching works? We get ideas from others and adapt them to fit our needs.) The idea behind the letters is to have one-on-one interaction with students—a luxury not often afforded with a one-to-100 teacher-to-student ratio. Genny asks her students to write to her about themselves as readers, writers, learners, and teachers. While I do this sometimes as well, often I invite students to ask questions or talk about whatever they wish. It becomes a forum for an exchange of thoughts and ideas.

"You can't sweep other people off their feet, if you can't be swept off your own."
Clarence Day

When I write back to my students, I write in the margins, on the back of the pages, or wherever I can squeeze in a word. I have found that these letters offer students the opportunity to express their fears or concerns about becoming teachers. I don't know how many times I have written the words, "What you are feeling is very normal."

As a rule, I require four letters a semester, one a month. Students can turn in their letters any time during the month, so I receive a few each class period rather than 100 at once, which makes reading them much more enjoyable and not overwhelming.

The letters I receive from students are usually positive and encouraging to me as a teacher—in other words, they don't usually challenge my paradigms. Recently, however, I received a letter from a student who, as a physical education major, was quite angry that he had to take a reading class. The course, Reading and Writing in the Content Fields, is a requirement at our university for all education majors because reading and writing are involved in all subject areas. His letter began, "First of all, I want you to know that I think your class is the biggest waste of my time and money, and I think the only reason I have to take it is so the university can stick me for more money." His letter went on in this vein for a full page.

My first reaction was disbelief. How could a student have the gall to write to a teacher that way, especially at the beginning of the semester? I tried to think of the reaction some of my teachers might have had if I had written such comments to them. (I quickly shook that image from my mind.) My disbelief turned to anger. I was ready to write back and tell him that with an attitude like his, perhaps he should change professions—and classes. But that might have

"All our knowledge has its origins in our perceptions."
Leonardo da Vinci

been the expected reaction—he was probably looking for that response from me. I decided to opt for a different mind-set about this student. I invite openness and honesty in the "Dear Beth" letters, so I cannot criticize students for saying what they think. I wrote to him that I understood his feelings, that I could see how a physical education teacher would question the need for a reading class. Rather than attempting to convince him at that point that reading was important, I told him to relax, enjoy the class, and focus on learning how he could be a better physical education teacher, which I knew he must desire or he wouldn't be in the program. His attitude changed immediately. He became like a new student and actively participated in the class. He got to have his say, and that was all he needed. Henry Ford said, "If there is any one secret of success, it lies in the ability to get

"Every [person] takes the limits of his own field of vision for the limits of the world."
Arthur Schopenhauer

the other person's point of view and see things from his angle as well as from your own." The paradigm change for me was that I was able to see his viewpoint rather than interpreting his comments as a personal attack.

As a teacher, I have a certain paradigm about how students should act and how they should treat me. When a student doesn't fit that mold, I can either try to force him into my paradigm or I can change what I expect. I have a choice. It is my decision, and it all takes place within my mind. If I want to encourage my students to be open-minded thinkers, then I choose to allow them to express their feelings openly. Therefore, when my perceptions change, my students change. Sadker and Sadker (1994) stated, "When teachers change, so do their students." I have seen that happen over and over again in my classroom.

Who Says it Has to Be Done That Way?

Students leave college with new ideas and teaching philosophies they are eager to put into place in their own classrooms. Yet, when they embark on their careers, they often find themselves teaching the way they have been taught rather than the way they believe they should teach. This is one of the first great disappointments for many new teachers. One reason for this difficulty may be that, although they learned the theories, they were never shown how to apply them. When they are faced with the unknown, their fear of failure, combined with the intimidation of being new on the job, may cause them to let go of their ideals and revert back to what is familiar. Yet taking the risk to venture out in new directions and try new methods may be just the ticket some teachers need to stay enthused about teaching. According to Reutzel and Cooter (1992), "Teachers who continue to experiment and update their teaching strategies throughout their careers tend to have greater successes with student development and performance, usually experience fewer discipline problems in these energized classrooms, and enjoy the teaching profession rather than burning out."

Just because others are teaching a certain way, doesn't mean you have to.

Falling back on traditional methods may not necessarily be the result of their success but the sense of their familiarity. We may assume that if something is done a particular way, then there must be a good reason for it, when, in fact, there may not be. An old story illustrates this point:

A young woman cut off both ends of a ham before baking it. "Why do you do that?" asked her husband.

She replied, "That's how Mama always did it."

The question made her wonder, so she called her mother to ask.

Her mother answered, "I don't know why, but my mom always cut off both ends."

Finally, the woman called her grandmother, asking her why she always cut off both ends of her ham.

Her grandmother replied, "Because a whole ham won't fit in my pan."

"The most extraordinary thing about a really good teacher is that he or she transcends accepted educational methods."
Margaret Mead

If a traditional method is effective and serves a purpose, there is no reason to change; but if you look at something you do and can find no reason for doing it, then perhaps a reevaluation will help. Nelson Parke, a retired industrial arts teacher, has found that the question, "Who says it has to be done that way?" helps him evaluate what he is doing and why he is doing it.

"Before going into the field of teaching I was in heavy construction for several years. My introduction to what was then called industrial arts came in my college courses. When I started teaching, I taught as I was instructed in college. I had been taught that industrial arts was the 'study of industry,' and that is what I told my students. After a couple of years of teaching I took a hard look at what was going on in my classrooms.

The question, 'Is what the students are learning in class worth my life?' was perhaps my most sobering thought. I could go back into construction and make more money than I was in teaching, so, in effect, as a teacher I was spending my life for something other than money. There needed to be a reason for my being there. I selected a typical student in one of my classes and determined what that student had learned during the year. The typical project was constructing a coffee table or bookcase. The student learned to identify a few kinds of wood, how to measure, how to saw and join the edges of some boards, how to cut some joints, how to glue boards together, and how to sand and apply finish to those boards. There was a little more, but that was basically it. In reality he was not learning much for a year of work.

During the analysis I realized I had been lying to my students. We were not studying industry. The methods I was teaching them were not the methods industry would use. I was teaching home hobby shop. There was very little relationship between my class and industry. As the result of that analysis, I began to teach materials and processes more like industry would use.

In addition to the typical project work, we began to design projects to mass-produce like they do in industry. The students designed the product, made the necessary jigs and fixtures, and planned the production line. The development and planning took a lot of time. One year when they were ready to run the production line we asked teachers from other areas such as English and math to bring their classes to watch us in action. There was a lot of excitement among the students and it helped to publicize their work. The projects they made were sold to the public, and the students in the class kept the profits.

" . . . to be nobody but yourself in a world which is doing its best, night and day, to make you everybody else—means the hardest battle which any human being can fight, and never stop fighting."   e.e. cummings

As the students began to develop products, I found they knew very little about materials and processes used in industry. I began developing lab activities that used more materials and processes as used in industry. One of the activities was a candle holder. Typically a candleholder would be a piece of wood with some holes drilled in it. The wood would be sanded and a finish applied. The holder I designed to teach the students more about industry was made out of aluminum and copper. The pieces were round and formed to shape. In a typical class students used a compass to lay out the circles, then cut to shape by hand with tin snips. The rough edges have to be smoothed up with a hand file. The pieces are then formed by beating with a hammer. Doing the job properly takes considerable skill. After shaping, the piece is hand-sanded and polished, then riveted together.

I designed and built various tooling that allowed the students to use processes more typical of the industry. Now my students were really studying industry and using actual industry processes. Other industrial arts teachers around the country heard about what we were doing and asked me to help them set up their programs.

'Who says it has to be done that way?' Just because something has always been done a certain way does not make it the right way. Sometimes it is the blind leading the blind. I found I had to look at what I was teaching and make it more appropriate for what the students should be learning. The thing that kept me going over the years is that I was not only teaching my students the materials and processes used in industry, but I was helping shape this area of study for students and teachers around the country."

Progress, Not Perfection

Many of us were raised with a paradigm that we should always strive for perfection. We all know the sayings: "Anything worth doing is worth doing well" or "Do it right, or don't do it at all." We were taught that perfection is our goal. While that may not be a bad goal, it can be problematic for many of us because we are not happy unless we reach it. Perfection is not easily attainable, especially in teaching, because of the number of hours in the day, the number of students we have, and the endless demands placed upon us. If we are feeling pressured by our need for perfection, we can set ourselves free by changing our goal from perfection to progress. Progress is much more easily attained—for us and our students.

Every small breakthrough, each step of improvement, indicates progress; the road to success is progress.

Focusing on progress rather than perfection is something Beverly Newman learned years ago as a new teacher. She remembers that during her first year of teaching she would get very discouraged because she never felt like she had done enough. Something her principal told her then, 26 years ago, helped her deal with these pressures so common in teaching.

"As a new teacher I seemed to go home from school every day feeling as though I hadn't done enough. It wasn't just a feeling; I knew I hadn't done everything I had wanted to do. But no matter how hard I tried, I never got everything accomplished that I wanted to.

After one particularly discouraging day I stopped by my principal's office and told him my concerns. I never forgot what he told me. He said he would rather I go home every day feeling as though I could do more than to go home feeling I had done enough. He said too much self-satisfaction was dangerous. He helped me see that as teachers, there is always more we can do. There just aren't enough hours in the day; there's not enough of me to spread around to 35 kids.

"Perfectionism is a refusal to let yourself move ahead."
Julia Cameron

He helped me see that as long as I was doing my best then that was enough. While that helped me, it was still hard for me to accept. We're not making widgets on an assembly line. We are working with children's minds, emotions, their concepts of themselves. They are not machines. What we do, or don't do, counts.

I didn't go into teaching lightly. I never stopped striving for perfection, but I learned to live with acceptance of the progress I made."

We need to teach our students, also, to be encouraged with their progress. A commercial I (Ginny) have seen on television several times impresses me. It shows a young boy running a track and jumping hurdles. The hurdles are all set very low, and he easily jumps each one, running on to the next. The voice-over tells about the expectations we have for our children. The picture shows the youngster coming to a higher hurdle which, though difficult, is one he could jump. He comes to an abrupt stop. The voice says something about the challenges we give, or don't give, our children. If our expectations don't offer them reason to stretch, pretty soon they will not even try.

We teachers don't expect perfection in our students. But we do expect progress. One definition for perfection is "completeness" or "maturity." There is nothing wrong with striving for perfection in that sense. The way we will get there, and the way our students get there, is by taking one step at a time, one day at a time.

I remember when I learned how much I am motivated by seeing progress. I'd never realized it until I was doing some long-term substituting in a low-level special-education class years ago. I worked for over a week with one boy who was supposed to learn to identify the letter "F."

"Give up the quest for perfection and shoot for five good minutes in a row."
Cathy Guisewite, creator of the comic strip "Cathy"

Whether that was an appropriate goal for this child I don't know, but that was my assigned task. I was weary. Each day it was as if he had never seen the letter. He could not recognize it, and I had run out of ways to try to help him recognize it. I felt defeated because I desperately needed to see some progress, and I didn't.

Teachers are inspired by the progress of their students. Hazel Rathel taught for a number of years in southwest Georgia and says she thoroughly enjoyed the children with whom she worked. Many of them were under-privileged and lacked the things so often taken for granted.

"It was important for me to find ways that those children could have broader experiences that would not only help them with their schoolwork, but also add to their quality of life. I am vitally interested in these children having the same opportunities as others so they can succeed in the world. I was so excited to see the progress they made.

The progress I saw in these children was not limited to academics. New experiences broadened their knowledge of the world outside their own culture. One of the projects I planned to expand their horizons was to pair students in our school with foster grandparents from a retirement center and the county retirement home. We took the students by bus to these centers. Our students loved going to these centers where they wrote letters, played games, read to their 'grandparents,' gave plays or talent shows and had an annual social with them.

"It is true that we shall not be able to reach perfection, but in our struggle toward it we shall strengthen our characters and give stability to our ideas."
Confucius

Their parents cooperated and occasionally would take a foster grandparent out to dinner or do something special by keeping in contact.

Another activity along the same lines was to pair sixth-grade students with kindergarten students. The older children read books, played games, and were the 'big sister' or 'big brother' to the younger kids. The chief activity was to write a book about the kindergarten child and illustrate it. I was so excited to find this especially effective with some of our at-risk sixth graders who excelled at reading, writing, and illustrating their 'little brother or sister's' books.

I loved working with these students and it thrilled me to see the progress they made."

Billie Beckman teaches special education in Whittier, California, across the United States from Hazel Rathel, but she, too, has been motivated by the progress of her students. She has taught upper elementary, infants, and preschool in the special-education program of the public schools.

"I work with preschool children who are autistic and who have cerebral palsy and Down's syndrome. I have found that I have to work with the parents as much as I do their children. Some of these parents are in total denial. They are in a stage of grief, and they simply want me to fix their children. I try to show the parents as much kindness as possible. We have support groups for them and have all sorts of programs with very good speakers. As I work with the little children in my classes, it is rewarding to see parents making progress as well as the children. For them, progress means accepting the limitations of their children and allowing them the freedom to develop at their own pace."

"With time and patience, the mulberry leaf becomes satin."
Oriental Proverb

Marlene Breeze, a business education teacher for 19 years, finds it rewarding to go into the bank and other offices in her Oklahoma town and see her former students using the skills she taught them. Progress is important to her, but it's not only academic progress that counts for something. She remembers one of her students.

"I tried to write encouraging remarks or complimentary statements on papers I would return to let students know I noticed improvement and effort, much like elementary teachers put stickers or happy faces on papers. I kept trying to encourage one young lady because I knew she could do better. She came from a home situation that was difficult to say the least. I continued to encourage her, and finally, on one of her papers she handed in to me, she had written, 'I don't know why you care, no one else does.' She knew I cared, and I think students should know a teacher cares."

"Keep trying. It's only from the valley that the mountain seems high." Unknown

Gay Lynn Russell admits that she has loved being a school counselor for the past 20 years. Her school district evidently thought she was doing something right when they honored her with the Counselor of the Year award. She enjoys seeing her students' progress.

"I look for those steps the kids take. You don't have to take giant steps. You can take tiny steps to reach a goal. It's hard for us—let alone kids—to take giant steps. I remember one student who used to come into my office ranting and raving. She did not want to look at anyone else's side of a conflict. She did not want to think about it. She just wanted to go wild. I worked with her on conflict mediation. I gave her a form on which I had her write down her feelings, write about the conflict itself, and how she could resolve it. She finally got it figured out! One day she came in and said, 'Give me one of those sheets!' Now that was progress, and I was pleased. When I can see that I've helped someone take even a tiny step, I feel good."

Karen Stanley remembers the unfolding of self-confidence in one of her students.

"I had a very quiet student in my keyboarding class. If she spoke a word to me all year long, I could hardly hear her. She joined Future Business Leaders of America and began taking more business classes. As she became involved, I gave her opportunities for more and more responsibility within the organization, and she gradually started coming out of her shell, even running on the local level for FBLA president. Later, she went on to run for a district office.

"Before you can score you must first have a goal."   Unknown

She stood in front of a group of around 350 students to speak during the campaign. This was the same girl who two years before wouldn't utter a sound in class. This, in my opinion, was a victory. It didn't matter how the vote came out; she was a winner."

Mistakes are not Always Mistakes

When something we set out to do does not turn out the way we think it should, we call it a mistake. This is another paradigm we need to look at in evaluating our perspectives. Rather than looking at a mistake as a negative, we should consider trying to view it in a positive light. Perhaps if we look at the situation through a different lens, we will see that it may not have been wrong after all. It is important to allow ourselves the freedom to fail, because sometimes the things we identify as mistakes turn out to be some of our greatest teaching tools.

A mistake may be an asset rather than a liability.

Several years ago as a new teacher, I (Beth) tried a reading activity I had experienced as a student in high school. Remembering an enjoyable English class where we all had read and discussed the same book, I decided I would plan the same thing for my fifth and sixth split-grade class. I now know using literature sets to teach reading is a tried and true method, but at the time I had never heard of anyone using anything other than basals. After ordering 30 copies of *Gentle Ben*, we read the book as a class. Although the reading went fairly well, the

*"Name the greatest of all the inventors: Accident."
Mark Twain*

method did not take into account the many different ability levels in my class. The next time I bought five or six copies each of several different books and planned to let the students read in groups.

The day these new books arrived, my students were so excited. After giving a short introduction to each of the books, I told my students we would divide into groups. Hands went up immediately, and students asked if they could read with their friends. I really didn't mind, and I told them so, but as soon as I saw them grouping themselves, I realized I had made a big mistake. One group contained the slowest reader in the class and her best friend, an avid reader. I had learned in my college classes that reading groups needed to be formed according to reading levels, so I was sorry I had let the students group themselves. But I was a person of my word, and I decided this time I would let them read with whom they wanted. Next time, though, they would be in assigned groups.

"The [person] who never makes any mistakes, never makes anything." Maltbie Babcock

An amazing thing happened. The two girls I was concerned about quickly read their first book and came looking for another. They made trips to the library together and read book after book. My mind was changed. After seeing these two girls' excitement about reading, in spite of the vast difference in their reading levels, as well as the enthusiasm of the rest of the class, I continued to let students group themselves. Groups were selected according to the books they wanted to read.

It pleased and surprised me to see that what I had originally thought was a mistake turned out to be a good teaching strategy. Students enjoyed books more because they were choosing books that interested them, and they were allowed to read them with their friends. Even though I still used the basal to teach reading skills, I let the students read with their groups every day just for the pleasure of reading.

Years later an even more amazing thing happened. One night three of my former students came to visit me. They were selling candy to support their upcoming high school band trip. They stayed for two hours while we reminisced about the two years they had spent in my class. We had such fun I invited all three of them to come talk to my preservice teachers at the university where I now teach a reading class. They told stories about their experiences in my class, and then I asked my students if they had any questions for the girls. I panicked when one of my students asked how the girls felt about ability grouping. I had learned a lot about reading since my days as a new teacher, and I now regretted my method of the traditional three groups and round-robin reading.

"It is necessary to learn from others' mistakes. You will not live long enough to make them all yourself." Hyman Rickover, U.S. Navy Admiral

I looked at those three girls: Stacey (names have been changed), a low reader; Meagan, one of the best readers I had ever had; and Susan, who read on grade level. I was afraid Stacey would say that I had scarred her for life. I almost fell out of my chair when she was the first to speak up and say, "Oh, I loved the groups! I was in the high one." Then the other two girls chimed in and said the same thing. How could that be? That wasn't the way it was.

I didn't hear anything else that was said during that class period because I was racking my brain trying to figure out why each girl thought she was in the high group. Then it dawned on me. When they thought of "reading groups," they were thinking of the groups where they read together for pleasure every day. What an impact that had on me! After class, I couldn't wait to find out what kinds of readers they were now as seniors in high school. Ashley, the low reader, said she loves to read. Her favorite books are Agatha Christie novels. Susan, the average reader, said she has read every single book in the *Goosebumps* series. She said she knows they are too easy for her, but she loves them and can't wait for the new ones to come out. Meagan, the avid reader, still continually has a book in her hands as she did in elementary school.

What invaluable lessons were reinforced for me that day: It is a good reading practice to let students read with friends because they have shared interests; it's important for teachers to make time for students to read books together every day because practice means progress; it's true that students' attitudes toward reading are crucial to their success as readers; and it's okay to make mistakes. The "mistake" I made in telling my students they could read with their friends ended up being one of the best things I did as an elementary teacher.

Sometimes keeping our minds focused on our misdirected goals prevents us from seeing the reality. Nelson Parke had a lifelong dream of being an inventor. When he became a teacher, he thought he was giving up his dream.

"I like to design and build things. You might call it inventing or problem solving. When I decided to be a teacher I thought one of the benefits of being an industrial arts teacher would be having the access to the equipment and time in the summers to follow that bent of my personality.

I began to develop a program for my classes. Lab activities had to be developed; manuals had to be written and tested, then rewritten; special tooling had to be designed, made, tested, and refined. I taught part-time in the summers and the program I was developing took so much time I did not have time to 'invent.' I was disappointed.

After many years of teaching I arrived at school one morning, and as I walked through the storage area where the special tooling was stored, a realization struck me. All these years I had been disappointed that I had not had time to invent, yet there on those shelves were about 125 different tools I had invented, tested, and refined for my students! I had been doing what I wanted all along and had not realized the thing I thought was keeping me too busy to invent was actually my golden opportunity.

"A mistake is not something to complain about, or to be ashamed of. It is a great teacher." Norman Vincent Peale

As a youth I remember the story of a little girl who lived on a hill on the eastern side of a valley. In the morning sun she could see a house across the valley that had golden windows. It was beautiful. She wished she could live in such a wonderful house. She dreamed of a closer view of the house with the beautiful golden windows. When she grew older her parents let her walk the long distance across the valley to see the house. One morning she packed a lunch and set out. When she reached her destination that afternoon, she found that the house did not have golden windows; they were just as plain as the windows on her house. Disappointed, she set out for home.

As she headed home late in the afternoon, she looked across the valley at her house and was quite surprised to see that it had golden windows. You see, in the morning the sun was in the east and would shine on the windows in the west. She and the sun were now in the west and the sun was shining on her windows.

Sometimes we have the very things we desire but do not recognize that fact. And sometimes what we view as life mistakes are not really mistakes at all. A reality check of what you have might be in order. You might be living in the house with the golden windows."

Moment by Moment

You've been there. We all have. You have planned a flawless lesson and have spent hours organizing activities to correlate. The time has come, and students' eyes are on you . . . mostly. Somehow, learning the correct usage of verbs just doesn't seem to excite them. Suddenly, interrupting your explanation, a fire truck speeds by, sirens blaring. A student jumps up, shouting, "Have you ever saw such a racket?" What do you say? Do you tell the kid to sit down and hush while you recite the correct conjunction of the verb "see"?

That spontaneous time in the classroom when life itself brings the lesson is your friend. Embrace it.

If you are a teacher who is inspired by the moment, you will look at the fire truck episode as an opportunity for teaching rather than as an interruption. It is easy to concentrate so much on the planned lesson that we put blinders on to anything that happens around us. After all, there is more to get done than we can accomplish. Time pushes. The public pushes. Businesses push. The state pushes. Skills must be taught, and we hear from all sides that we are failing at this. So we push, too. And by doing so, we trap ourselves and our curriculum in a box. Recognize that you can use the moment to teach. Thus, you may be able to get something across to your students that they otherwise would miss. When a student asks a question you can't answer, take advantage of the situation by creating a teachable moment.

"When you are a teacher you are always in the right place at the right time. There is no wrong time for learning. It may be the wrong time for what the teacher had planned to teach, but just as certainly it will be the perfect time to teach something else. Teachers learn to grasp the moment. Any time a student is there before you, the possibility is present, the moment is yours."
Betty B. Anderson

As a teacher in a split fifth- and sixth-grade classroom, one of my (Beth's) science objectives was to teach my students how to make magnets. I began with a large box of the necessary supplies and a one-page direction sheet for making magnets, which I had never made. The class was divided into groups and all of us were working on our magnets. When the students were not having much success, they did what students do—they asked for help. All I could say was, "I'm having trouble getting mine to work, too. Let's just keep trying." Then out of the chatter of voices, one group stood up and shouted, "It works! It works!" We all made a mad dash to their table to see how they had done it. I was at the front of the line.

That group explained to the rest of us what we had missed on the direction sheet. They told us we had to read direction number three carefully. So we all went back to our desks, read the directions more closely, and got our magnets to work. The group that was the first to get theirs working, without any direction from me, divided up and moved around the room helping others. The room was filled with excitement. It was an incredible day—one I will never forget. What do you think I did the next year when I taught that lesson? I did what I thought a good teacher should do. I told my students to read direction number three carefully or their magnets would not work. That may not have been my best choice. The magnets all worked the first time and the students were excited, of course, but the level of excitement was not the same as it had been the year before. There really is something to that idea of self-discovery; it works. I learned that I need to follow the moment. If I don't know an answer, it's okay. Sometimes when we don't know an answer, it becomes a challenge for our students to find it before we do, thereby creating a positive learning experience for them. And for us.

Since Ruth Skelton retired from teaching, she now works in business with her husband and says that together they put in about 100 hours a week. "Even though it is somewhat stressful and physically hard, it is not as hard as teaching, but I loved my 25 years of teaching." Ruth learned to appreciate those impromptu times in her classroom when a teachable moment just fell into her lap. Many such times occurred, but one in particular stands out.

"I was teaching the parts of fish by pointing out the fins on a red-tailed shark I had purchased purposely for the lesson. A student had brought in a crawdad that morning, and having no other place to put it, we put it in the aquarium. Just as I pointed out the dorsal fin, the crawdad made a meal of the shark, destroying my teaching tool! Of course, I went immediately to the topic of the food chain, asking what, in this case, the predator would be. I had to admit that I didn't even know crawdads ate fish!"

Cindy Nevins has taught fifth grade for 12 years. Her students told her recently that one thing they like about her is that if she finds out they don't know about something, she will leave her lesson plans for a time to teach them. She shares one such time.

"We were reading the book *Rascal* by Sterling North together in class. The story takes place in North America in 1916, and some of the characters were collecting aluminum. My students didn't understand why they would be having paper drives or collecting the aluminum. When I began to explain the reasons in relationship to World War I, I discovered that many of them didn't even know there had been a World War I.

I went into a study of that time period with them. We went to the library and did some research, and we discussed the stamp rationing and the pride

"I've learned that change occurs every five minutes in teaching, so it is essential not to be rigid." Rhonda Leeper, Elementary Teacher

the people of the United States had for their country. Many of the students went home asking questions of their parents about the war. Of course, some of them got answers regarding World War II, but at least they were asking questions at home. This was an interesting side study for all of us, and it began with our reading the book *Rascal*."

Fuel for the Fire
IDEAS TO INCORPORATE

- When faced with frustration because your teaching methods do not coincide with your educational philosophies, try asking yourself, "Who says it has to be done that way?" Set aside one day to pay close attention to what you do in the classroom. Ask yourself specific questions about why you do what you do. For example, why do put your desk where it is? Why do you structure your classroom the way you do? Why do you take roll the way you do?

- If you do find something in your style of teaching that does not coincide with your beliefs, don't feel you have to immediately revamp the way you teach. Begin slowly. Is there something simple you can do today that will fall more closely in line with your philosophies about how children learn best?

- Recognize your students' progress and celebrate it by creating a special display near the school office.

- Recognize your own progress and celebrate it. Treat yourself.

- Create opportunities for all students to succeed at something. For example, in a class discussion, ask some students lower-level questions that you know they will be able to answer. Everyone needs to feel success in some area, and when students feel they are making progress, it motivates them, which, in turn, will motivate you.

- When you feel as though you have made a mistake in your teaching, wait for a brief period to judge whether it really was a mistake. Write down the "pros" and "cons." Don't be too quick to judge your actions.

- If something occurs in the news locally, nationally, or internationally that you can tie into a lesson, incorporate it into your plans.

- Listen to your students. Take advantage of situations that arise that may correlate with your planned lesson. Let your lessons incorporate your students' interests. With practice, you can learn to make anything fit into what you are teaching.

- Look again at your dreams and aspirations. Make a list of your aspirations and see how many of those dreams you have fulfilled. Look carefully because sometimes we achieve our dreams in ways different from what we expected.

Just for the Preservice Teacher

- On the left side of a page, make a list of classroom situations you faced as a student that you would like to change in your own classroom. On the right side of the page, make a corresponding list of how you want to handle those same situations differently.
- Write about how your views on education have changed since you made the decision to become a teacher.

Change of Action Facilitates Change in Attitude

"Action seems to follow feeling, but really action and feeling go together; and by regulating the action, which is under the more direct control of the will, we can indirectly regulate the feeling, which is not."
William James

Change can occur in different ways. Often we begin by changing the way we think; other times it is easiest first to change our actions. An old axiom, "Act as if" is one we can put into practice when change does not come easily. In some cases, we may know we need to change our actions but we don't feel ready. Educational researcher Martens (1992) found that even when teachers see a change as desirable, they can still experience ambivalent feelings toward the change because they may feel a loss of control over an area in which they felt competent. When this happens we can act as if we are competent and ready. When we go ahead and make changes in what we do, chances are our attitudes will follow.

Decades ago, William James of Harvard said, "Action seems to follow feeling, but really action and feeling go together; and by regulating the action, which is under the more direct control of the will, we can indirectly regulate the feeling, which is not. Thus the sovereign voluntary path to cheerfulness, if our cheerfulness be lost, is to sit up cheerfully and to act and speak as if cheerfulness were already there." When we know we need to make a change but we don't feel ready, we have to take an active step—we have to do something.

Person Working Equals Person Learning

One area of teaching with which we all struggle is putting in many more hours in preparing, planning, teaching, and grading than our students do in learning. We understand that the workload is out of proportion, but we don't know how to change. In this situation, a change of attitude may not help. We can try not to resent the hours we spend outside of our classrooms, but that doesn't change the reality. This situation calls for a change of action. But what action?

If you are the one doing most of the work in your classroom, then you are the one doing most of the learning.

I (Beth) once heard a saying that directly answers this question and has had a profound impact on my teaching, and according to my pre-service teachers, has an important effect on them as well. The saying is, "The person who is doing most of the work in the classroom is the person who is doing most of the learning." When I first heard this adage, I didn't like it too much. I was afraid it sounded like the teacher was trying to get out of doing work. But as I do with most new ideas I think are worth pursuing, I put the concept to the test.

My first chance to try out this new theory came while I was writing a midterm test. After working a long period of time, I stopped and asked myself, If it's true that the person doing most of the work is the person doing most of the learning, then how can I turn this process around to help my preservice teachers? I thought about what processes we teachers go through to write a test. First, we review the material in our textbook, lecture notes, and/or lesson plans. Then we choose what we think is the most important information—what we think the students should have learned. From that list we formulate questions that are clear and concise and measure what we want to measure. Once that is accomplished, we type the questions, proofread and edit the test, make copies, and, finally, after students have taken the test, we grade them and record the scores.

"Remember, your students should work harder than you do."
Gwen Jeffries,
High School Librarian

This is a long and tedious process that has helped us review the material and plant it firmly in our minds. A test that took me hours to write may take my students just 30 minutes to complete. If my students had developed their own exam, they would have benefited a great deal from reviewing, determining important points, and formulating appropriate questions.

After thinking through all this, I decided to try a little experiment. I told my students to come to class the following week prepared to tell me everything they had learned so far in class. I told them I wanted to know what was already in their heads, not what they would have to cram to memorize the night before. When the day arrived, I was nervous. I asked myself, What if I stand in front of my students asking, "What have you learned?" and they look at me with blank faces? What if they haven't learned as much as I have hoped? Then what am I going to do?

I was amazed at what happened. My students bombarded me with facts so fast that I had trouble writing all of them on the board. They initiated discussions about what they had learned. The class even thought of things I hadn't. As I looked back over their list, I sighed a big sigh of relief realizing they had learned what I had taught.

I have found that if I keep the question, How can I turn this around so that the students are doing most of the work? in the back of my mind, it improves my teaching and my students' learning. Not only do students learn more, but my time is freed up somewhat so that I can be more of an active participant/learner. Each semester several students comment on course evaluations that one of the most beneficial lessons they learned in our class was that "the person working equals the person learning."

Cathy Carleton tells about how this principle worked in her classroom.

"In one of the schools where I taught, I felt strongly about the need to develop a recycling program. Rather than telling the students my thoughts, I developed a unit that dealt with solid waste. We read and saw films and had discussions, dealing with the amount of solid waste, and what things were contained therein that could be recycled. Soon, one of the students suggested that we should consider a recycling campaign. We discussed it as a class and several of them added ideas and volunteered for some role within the project. The class unanimously voted to pursue the plan and began organizing themselves into groups that would deal with the multiple aspects involved. The project was a great success, including an all-school assembly to kick off the campaign. The assembly was covered by local media and the students wrote cheers and rap songs to get the rest of the school involved. The point is, it was the students' idea, so they were willing to put forth the effort to make it happen. Be creative with your approach and they'll pick up on the logical conclusion. Give them some credit for insight and allow them to take pride in their ideas."

Before Gwen Jeffries became a junior high and high school librarian, she taught Spanish for several years. She learned from the perspective of a foreign language teacher that for her students truly to benefit, it was important for her to remember that they must work harder than the teacher does. She explains what she means by this statement.

"I learned in my techniques classes that students learn from writing the questions. This is not busy work, but it is work to focus the mind. I don't think this is taught anymore, but I think it is very important. We shouldn't be running the copy machine to death. Students get reinforcement from doing some copying from what they see. On worksheets, students often mindlessly fill in the blanks. The idea of following patterns is important. When we have to write the question we see, I think it ingrains patterns in our thought processes. Children learn from doing. If I spend all of my time writing questions for the Electronic Bookshelf (a computer program developed to test comprehension of books students have read), and then keying them into the computer, I am doing the work. Why not have a student make up the test questions? Why not have a student put them into the computer? They will be doing the work, and they will be doing the learning."

Freedom from Boredom

If we reach a point in our careers when we become bored with teaching, it is vitally important for us to take action. If you are an alert teacher, you will recognize when your tank is running low on motivation, and you are starting to get bored. When boredom strikes, it is time for change. You need to look for new ways to stimulate yourself. It may mean a new project. It may mean more learning for yourself, or breaking from long-established teaching molds to invent new ones. It may mean changing your physical surroundings. It may simply mean opening your eyes to what is around you. The key is action.

Your personal motivation creates energy, which revives your teaching and prevents boredom.

Something motivated us to teach in the first place or we wouldn't be where we are. That motivation may be as simple as a paycheck. One teacher says, "Of course, I do it for the money. I have a family to raise and the income is necessary." More often than not, however, more is involved than just the monthly check. As mundane tasks and constant demands pile up, the memory of our original motivation is often hidden under the load.

David R. Wright worked for 20 years simultaneously as a college and university teacher and as a member of the Pennsylvania House of Representatives. He says,

"When I get bored with teaching, I try to ask myself why I am bored. Then I wonder if I am bored because I am boring. I think often about the aphorism that there are no uninteresting subjects, there are only uninterested people. My theory is that what interests me may not interest students, but what does not interest me surely will not interest students. At times like that, I begin to rework the course, add new material, and strive to get more student involvement. I sometimes find that going to a conference or workshop, not necessarily one directly connected to my discipline, will spark in me a new interest. I find it stimulating and renewing to see good people perform whatever their discipline. Sometimes it works, sometimes it doesn't. Sometimes I have a great class; sometimes I wonder why they or I even bothered to show up. But the beauty and glory of teaching is that at the end of the year or the end of the semester there is a new beginning. For the teacher, there is always 'the land of beginning again.'"

> *"The cure for boredom is curiosity. There is no cure for curiosity."*
> Unknown

Bob Brady, a high school German teacher, enriches his own life through traveling in the United States and in Europe. He is constantly on the lookout for news events, items of interest, or tidbits of information that he can use in his classes. He reads the newspaper with one hand holding the paper and the other holding a pair of scissors, just in case he runs across an appropriate article.

"We have a lot of freedom in our job that people in others don't have—the freedom to change things. I try to think of something that's different than what we've been doing—like going outside to practice the language. Sometimes we watch videotapes students from previous years have made, or we might role-play. We have made videotapes that we've sent overseas, where we, for example, bring in a photo of a pet and discuss it for the partner school in Germany. We send cards or letters to our own school's previous foreign exchange students. I stay motivated by trying to find something radically different than a textbook exercise."

Monica Andrews has taught special education for 13 years. Her mind is always busy as she thinks of ways to keep herself and her students interested. She wrote and received an Incentives for Excellence in Education state grant which provided her classroom with a computer and the means to begin a publishing business. She and her middle and high school students named their business The Paper Company. They design and publish business cards, stationery, calendars, signs, and greeting cards. Students must calculate expenses, do inventory, reorder necessary materials, make out sales tickets, and deliver their products. Actual class time is used, as this is part of her classroom curriculum. The money students make is recycled into the company. Students in Monica's class have also written their own English textbook. With information from their teacher about what skills must be included, the students constructed their textbook exercises. The final project was their third-quarter grade.

Another project Monica has started is a program designed to help students with the transition from school to life outside school. She arranges to take students to clean houses. Teachers within the system have enthusiastically volunteered their homes as training grounds. Students earn money while learning to clean, and they recently saw the results of their efforts when they purchased their own vacuum cleaner with their earnings. These are activities that not only motivate her students but also help keep Monica interested in teaching. She says,

"Each new hour holds new chances for new beginnings."
Maya Angelou

"Sometimes it is difficult to stay motivated as a special-education teacher. I like change occasionally. For instance, I move the furniture in my classroom several times a year. It stirs things up a bit. I also try not to take my work home. I would rather stay late a few nights a week or work at school on a Saturday. This helps keep my home life separate. One other thing I enjoy doing is organizing. To do this I usually go to an office supply store and buy the latest desk trays or whatever looks different. It gives me a good reason to go through all that stuff that piles up on the desk every few weeks."

Mary Wright is motivated by creating units that are exciting to her and then seeing her junior high students find an interest in the "real-world" connection.

"I have become aware of times when my regular teaching format has become stale and outdated. Because of that, I have often changed the way a subject was presented. For example, my enthusiasm for shopping spilled over into the classroom as a shopping unit that made it easier for the students to realize there was indeed a relationship between what we do in class and in the real world.

Since I love to shop, I wrote a unit that developed into a study on money management. This proved very effective in the teaching of spending and saving, while teaching them the practical use of decimals, percentages, check writing, graphing, and other skills. Students were asked to bring a copy of the ad section of Wednesday's paper. A local bank furnished checkbooks with deposit slips and registers. I assigned all students the same salary as well as a budget I had already prepared. The budget contained expenses that would be typical of a household such as a house payment, car payment, health and car insurance, charity, groceries, department store items, and emergency expenses. I either listed a cost for each item

"To be interesting, be interested."
Mrs. Charles Northam Lee

or provided a means for the students to figure the cost. For example, for the charity giving, I told students to figure 10 percent of their salary.

For the groceries, I used a list I had previously prepared, which would be typical of a weekly grocery list. I found products I wanted them to purchase from the newspaper. I gave them a list of the items along with the store from which they were to 'purchase' them. They found the items in the newspaper, wrote down the prices, added the total, and calculated an appropriate rate of sales tax. They then used their checks to write a check to the store. After all 'purchases' had been made and all 'bills' paid, students turned in their checks, register, and their budget summary to me to be graded. Probably because of my own excitement and enthusiasm, this unit became a favorite, and in most cases, one of the units with the least behavior problems among students. It brought motivation to me because I learned I could create my own project and not only bring joy to myself and the students but also create a situation where more learning took place and fewer problems existed."

Exchange Challenges for Rewards

A classroom without challenges does not exist. The struggles we face as teachers may vary—and in fact they will vary—but they are always there just the same. Ask any teacher about the frustrations of the job and you won't have to wait long for detail after detail. Whether or not a challenge can be turned into a reward may depend on the action we take.

We can allow problems to pull us down or use them to pull us up.

I (Ginny) have learned that it is better for my own mental health and satisfaction if I can identify a particular frustration and then focus on the choices I have in dealing with it. Sometimes I just have to let go of the problem, realizing that there is nothing I can do about it. At one time, I found myself teaching in an area where for a variety of reasons my department had a very high turnover of teachers within a few years. This naturally weakened our program, which concerned me. At one point, a teacher was hired who was competently doing the job he was trained to do, but at the end of his first year he was not offered a contract for the following year. This was extremely frustrating to me because I knew how important consistency was in developing a strong program. However, there was absolutely nothing I could do to change the situation. I could express my opinion to the administration, which I did, but beyond that I could do nothing. My best option was to let go of it and concentrate on those things over which I had some control.

On the other hand, some problems may cause me to see that I need to change directions in my own life, such as making a change within my job, seeking ways to use my creativity, reevaluating my goals, or changing a preconceived idea. I have found that I can deal with a problem by changing my thinking, by seeking to turn the challenge into a reward.

I taught school several years ago in a minimum security prison where I worked with inmates who were studying for their GED, as well as with those who needed basic skills. I was surprised, and a bit apprehensive I must admit, when I found that a tutor had been assigned to help me, a prisoner who was serving a sentence for his involvement in a murder. I was unsure of how to approach both the inmate and the situation. I decided to ignore my feelings of anxiety and move forward. Calvin was very bright and was energetic in his work. We spent time talking as I shared the goals I had for the men in my class. Calvin became a protector of sorts for me, not in a physical sense, but he could foresee where problems might arise with certain inmates, and he would head them off. Whereas before I had to prove myself and take care of insubordinate attitudes as they arose, he began nipping them in the bud, as Barney Fife would say. Working with this man had seemed like an immense challenge when I began, but when Calvin found that he had been accepted for a work release program and began making preparations to leave, I realized how much of a blessing he had become to me in my teaching.

> "The gem cannot be polished without friction, nor a [person] be perfected without trials."
> Chinese proverb

Lori Elliott views students who have previously been a challenge for other teachers as an opportunity for her to make a difference.

"One year I had a boy who had a reputation for being a behavior problem, but I don't like to put much stock in what students have done before they come to my class. I want to let them start out fresh in my room. I believed in Brian and worked hard to help him believe in himself. I looked very hard to find his strengths, and then I made sure to let him know I noticed his every success. I tried to look past the behavior problems and see Brian. And I helped him see who he was by telling him what he did well and by pointing out to him what he could do.

By the end of the year he was on the A-B honor roll for the first time. He did so well. Even his scores on the achievement test went up. He couldn't believe how much he had changed.

Then Brian found out he was moving. He cried as we stood in the hall on his last day. He said, 'Mrs. Elliott, nobody understands me like you do.' Then I cried. I guess our job as teachers is to look beyond the facade the students have learned to show the world, and search with all of our hearts for the good within them that we know is there. Then we help them see it. Sometimes that's all they need. You hope they leave your room different than when they came in."

Judy Just, who has been teaching fourth grade for 27 years, doesn't let those students who are challenges fall through the cracks.

"I don't know why, but ornery little boys often become very endearing to me and have a special place in my heart, even though they can drive me crazy and make me want to pull out my hair. I try to think of ways to reach them such as finding out what their hobbies and interests are and talking to them about those things. For example, if a student wears a Dallas Cowboys football jacket to school, I will be sure to ask him about the game if the Cowboys played over the weekend.

I also find that using a lot of humor with them is effective. I laugh at their jokes and joke back with them. Also, the more agitated and upset they become, the calmer and more soft-spoken I have to be. Sometimes that is a real challenge for me. When I see these boys years later, it is always a very positive experience."

Tracey Hankins recalls a student who entered her room with a history of behavior problems, but left a changed young man.

"*O*ne of my students, whom I will call Alex, spent the first and second grades in lots of trouble. I was told he spent as much time in the principal's office as he did in the classroom. He was a child of an alcoholic and a drug addict mother who had sent him to live with his grandmother after telling him she didn't want him. Alex began the year in my room with an invisible wall between himself and everyone else. He did not let anyone inside his 'space.' His grandmother loved him very much, but she was battling her own personal challenge to beat the cancer that had spread throughout her body. Alex, deeply concerned about his grandmother, once asked me, 'What will happen to me when my grandma dies? My mother doesn't want me.'

"The more difficult the obstacle, the stronger one becomes after hurdling it."   Unknown

I befriended Alex by standing near him at recess or other times and chatting with him. I wanted him to know that I was there for him if he wanted to talk to me. Finally, he learned he could trust me. Soon he began opening up to others too. By the end of the year, Alex was giving up one recess a day to help the art teacher work with second graders, and another recess to tutor a fourth grader. Alex learned the value of giving. He touched my life in a very special way."

A reward of teaching that Deanne Camp, who has been teaching for 20 years, enjoys is seeing her students turn their failings or mistakes into opportunities for improvement.

"*S*everal years ago I had a student, Danny, a very active third grader, who would daily challenge my patience and understanding. His peers were often not accepting of him because he did not dress like them, behave like them, or have the same kinds of toys they had. I could see that his class disruptions were attempts to get attention from me and his classmates. Although Danny would give me a run for my money during the day, there were many mornings when he would walk in our classroom door and come up and hug me. I believed it was his way of apologizing without actually saying he was sorry. One morning he said, 'Don't you remember yesterday when I . . .' I told him, 'Yes, I remember yesterday, but nothing can be done to change yesterday; so let's start today as though nothing happened.

"Every problem is an opportunity in disguise."   Unknown

It is a new day and a chance for a new beginning.' Danny smiled and sat down. Did he challenge me that day as well? Of course, but I believe he always entered the classroom after that a little more sure of himself and perhaps a little more eager to learn because he knew I accepted him just the way he was. I felt that the other students became more accepting of him as well because they saw I cared for him just as he was.

New beginnings are important at every grade level. I once had a college student I'll call Angela who used her notes during the first exam of the semester. The exam was not an open book/note test. I knew what she was doing but allowed her to finish the exam. When she turned in her test I asked to speak to her privately in the hall. She gave me an excuse for why she had used her notes and was very embarrassed. I tossed out that exam and gave her a different one. She went on to do extremely well in my class and became a wonderful teacher and an excellent role model for her students.

The idea that every day is a new beginning still permeates my teaching. That philosophy has remained constant whether teaching first graders or first-grade teachers. When we give students a second chance, or third chance, or fourth chance, we are helping them face the challenges of becoming the kind of individuals they know they can become."

Fuel for the Fire
IDEAS TO INCORPORATE

- Look closely at what you spend your time on away from school. Are you doing work your students could do as a learning exercise? For example, if you are developing a worksheet to reinforce something you have taught, why not put your students into groups and, providing guidelines, have them make the worksheets. Then have the groups trade and work each other's. This allows for a great deal of review of the material.

- If you presently feel bored with your job, spend some time thinking of ways you can awaken your own interest. Plan to put at least one new idea into operation in your classroom this week. For example, if you have been dreaming about taking a trip to Europe, plan a unit for your students to study interesting places to visit there.

- Do some serious "housecleaning" in your room. Freshen it up. Change things around.

- Identify the challenges you face. Try to determine if there is a way you can turn them into rewards by changing your own thinking, applying some creativity.

- Think of the past. Recall instances when you have dealt with a frustration in such a way that it became a positive thing for you.

- Look around you. Are there people with whom you work who make lemonade from lemons? Talk with them. Ask them to share with you just exactly how they make that happen.

- Make a regular time for yourself, perhaps first thing in the morning, when you can have a quiet time. Read something that will inspire you or remind you to think positively. Begin your day with the attitude that you will look for good in the things that happen around you.
- Establish a plan that will guide you in dealing with your challenge. Follow it. For example, if you have a student who is causing you problems, make a list of things you can do to work with that student such as making sure to find at least one thing positive about him or her, looking for a success so you can write an encouraging note, or making an effort to write positive comments on his or her papers.
- If you have a student who is causing behavior problems in your room, make it a personal goal to be the teacher who reaches that child. Force yourself to look deeply for the good in the child and then try to build on those strengths.
- Don't be too quick to wish your challenges gone. They are the catalysts that force you to stretch. Concentrate on the spark that was, and still is, inside you; that one that said to you, you are a teacher.

Just for the Preservice Teacher

- Plan an activity that incorporates one of your interests. For one of your college assignments, write a unit plan on a subject of special interest to you.
- If you are getting bored with school or discouraged about the years you have invested in preparing to be a teacher, make a list of the reasons you chose this profession. Tape your list to your refrigerator or put it in a place where you see it often to remind you to "hang in there."

Change Your Emotions by Changing Your Mind-Set

Our emotions play a major role in how we view teaching, students, and learning.

Our emotional well-being as teachers is an important factor in preventing burnout. Therefore, we need to have an understanding of our emotional makeup. According to Garrett, Sadker, and Sadker (1994), "If teachers are to create an environment that is conducive to personal growth, they must first explore their own feelings about themselves and their students." Cooper (1994) stated, "There is evidence from psychology that persons who deny or cannot cope with their own emotions are likely to be incapable of respecting and coping with the feelings of others. If teachers are to understand and sympathize with their students' feelings, they must recognize and understand their feelings."

Teaching is a profession where our emotions run strong. We feel passionately about what we do, and our students can evoke feelings in us ranging from intense compassion to anger. How we deal with those emotions has a profound impact on our job satisfaction. For us to remain fulfilled in our careers we need to look for ways to build upon those emotions that make us stronger and let go of those that drag us down. As we do this, we will enjoy our jobs more and our students will benefit as well.

Laughter is a Stress Killer

It is easy to dwell on things that frustrate us. If we look hard enough, we can always find a disgruntled parent to face or a student who simply refuses to cooperate, and it seems to be a constant battle to stay ahead of the problems. Maybe you have successfully jumped that hurdle of focusing on the positive, but you find yourself up against another one—that of delving so deeply into your work that you become consumed by it.

Don't bury the humor that sneaks up on you in the classroom.

Committee meetings to attend, papers to grade, curriculum to write, classes to take, events to coach, conferences to hold, ball games to attend, clubs to sponsor—and these are all things in addition to actually teaching.

Whoa, Nellie! How do we hold on to our sanity? One tested and proved method is to learn to laugh at situations that arise, rather than becoming stressed by them. According to Norman Cousins in *The Healing Heart*, laughter not only aids healing in the body but also tends to block deep feelings of apprehension and panic.

I (Ginny) remember a time during a very difficult job situation which was lightened by laughter. The first year at my present job was truly a nightmare. I was hired in October after two teachers had quit and a string of substitutes refused to come back. The main lesson I taught that year was that I would be back. One day I was talking to my students, and I moved to my desk to look at something. I leaned back to sit down, totally missed the chair, and landed smack dab in the middle of the floor. A thousand thoughts went through my head as I was heading down, and when I finally landed; the main one was, How will I ever gain control of this class after this? I sat for what seemed like hours but was surely only seconds. The class was unnervingly silent. I finally peered my head up over my desk, grinned sheepishly, and told them it was okay to laugh. They looked at one another, and their laughter shook the classroom.

Time after time, situations arise that can give cause to laugh or cry. Will Rogers said, "I don't make jokes. I just watch the government and record the facts." Teaching can be like that. To find the humor in our classrooms, we don't need to make jokes, we can just pay attention to what goes on around us.

Rhonda Leeper tells of a situation when she had a choice of getting totally embarassed or choosing to smile.

"I was telling my first-grade students about my husband going wild boar hunting. One boy went home and announced at the dinner table that night, 'My teacher's husband went wild hoar hunting!' Was I ever glad I knew the family, and was able to laugh with them about their son's misinterpretation."

Carl Ochner is a new middle school teacher who found laughter was a good way to break the ice with his students.

"I had been advised by veteran teachers that I should be somewhat stern at the beginning of school. They told me that it is easier to start out strict and then loosen up than the other way around. So that's what I did. The first couple of weeks of school even the brightest students were scared to death of me. One day we were discussing different forms of energy and I could tell the students weren't quite getting it. I turned around to pick up a meterstick (don't they make yardsticks anymore?) to bang on the desk to make my point. As I grabbed the meterstick, I accidentally struck a piñata that was hanging from the ceiling which then fell on my head. Amid the uproarious laughter, I positioned the meterstick in Michael J. Fox fashion as he did in the amplifier scene from *Back to the Future*, and slid across the front of the room on my knees strumming the meterstick like a guitar.

"Every person is a darn fool for at least five minutes every day. Wisdom consists in not exceeding the limit." Elbert Hubbard

My students then learned the concept of sound energy, and they learned that I was not the stick-in-the-mud they thought I was."

Cindy Nevins remembers a first day of school that set the stage for an intimate atmosphere with her fifth graders. She giggles as she tells the story.

"We were doing first-day-of-school things. I was in front of the class explaining rules and so on. The kids in my class had not gotten to know me yet, of course. One little girl came up to me and said, 'Mrs. Nevins, I don't know if you know it or not, but your middle button is unbuttoned.' I looked down and saw my slip and part of my belly showing. I had been talking to them all that time with my dress open. What could I do? I just looked at the class and said, 'Well, guys, you're just going to have to help me stay dressed this year, I guess.' All I could do was laugh at myself and go on."

Bonnie Parrigon has found in her 20 years of elementary school teaching that laughter is what makes her classroom an enjoyable place to be.

"Not a day goes by in our classroom when we don't laugh about something. I want my room to be a happy place for both the students and me; in fact, we start each day by going around the room and the children say why they are happy. I can come to school with a heavy burden on my mind and before I know it, the burden is not quite so heavy. Students can be the best cures for what ails you. We find many things to laugh about.

"Angels can fly because they take themselves lightly."
Unknown

For example, one day the custodian came in to fix one of our bookcases. Shortly after he left the room, one of my students went to get the 'A' encyclopedia only to find that the custodian had accidentally screwed it to the bookcase. We joked about that for the rest of the year. It was like a private joke that only those in our class would understand.

For me, my students, and the teachers I work with, the days go so much more smoothly when we relax and enjoy laughing with one another."

Let Go of Fear

Fear can debilitate. It can hold us captive. In teaching, we will be faced with many things that frighten us. It may be a fear of failure, a fear of confrontation, a fear of miscommunication or misunderstanding. It may even be a fear of the kids in our classrooms. It is important to distinguish between fears that are genuine and those that are false. If, after close scrutiny, you are certain that your fear is valid, seek counsel from another teacher or administrator about how to deal with it.

Fear can rob us of the joys of today and the fruitfulness of tomorrow.

If you recognize that your fear is not valid, then make a choice to release it. William Jennings Bryan advised us to do the thing we fear and get a record of successful experiences behind us. When we do this we develop confidence in ourselves and in our ability to handle fearful situations with more ease.

When I (Ginny) was a little girl, I worried about everything. I remember walking past a den area in our home and watching my mother sort through paperwork. Since my father had died not long before, I was fretting about my own adult years: How will I ever understand enough about insurance to take care of it? How will I know what bills will need to be paid?

What if I have no husband and am left alone to figure these things out for myself? Pretty sobering thoughts for a ten-year-old. The trouble was, though the worries were real, the problems weren't.

Bill Gillham, founder of Lifetime Guarantee, tells the story of a man who finds himself awakened by the sound of a bear scratching and growling, trying to get into the cabin in which he is staying. The man is terrified. The cabin is very sturdily built; the door is extremely thick and bolted tightly. The man is safe. There is no way the bear can get into the cabin. But the man's feelings are the opposite. He does not feel safe. He could actually die of fright at the very time that he is in complete safety.

When my older son was five, I asked him to forgive me for something I had done. He said he forgave me, but he kept on complaining and worrying about it. I said to him, "Royce, when you forgive someone, you're not supposed to keep worrying and still be mad. You're supposed to give it up."

"I am?" he answered. "You never told me that part. Okay."

Perhaps you have never realized that you have to make a choice to let go of some of your fears. But it must be a conscious effort to say, I will not be held captive by that fear any longer.

Ann Werland, Spanish teacher of middle and high school students, tells of being a young city teacher coming to a small school.

"I had lots of fears. I remember thinking that everyone knows everyone in the school and the community, and I don't know anyone. The teachers were all older than I was. Will I be as good a teacher as they are? Will I measure up to their expectations? I was full of questions and had knots in my stomach.

One of the things that helped me most was what seemed at first to be a real obstacle. Our school was crowded, with no room available for me. I was assigned to travel from room to room to teach my Spanish classes. As I went into different teachers' rooms, I got to know them. I realized that my fear was unfounded, but I had to get to know the teachers to recognize it. I came to see that they all have their own way of teaching and do their own thing in the best way they know how. I could not worry about what they did. I had to concentrate on how to do my job the best way possible."

"My life has been filled with terrible misfortunes, most of which have never happened."
Michel de Montaigne

Tracey Hankins experienced a situation in which she had a valid fear, a fear all teachers are afraid they may have to face someday.

"After teaching kindergarten for a few years, I moved to fourth grade. While it was a wonderful experience overall, there was one time in particular that was not quite so wonderful. So that my students could learn to locate places they read about in newspaper articles, I made a large world map on a bulletin board. The students would share with the class the articles they had read and then, using a straight pin and a piece of string, they would put

"We lend power to the things we fear."   O.S. Marsden

up the article and run the string from the article to the location where the event occurred. This was proving to be a successful endeavor until one day, before I knew what was happening, one of my students had put the pin in his mouth and sucked it down his windpipe. I rushed him to the office, where we called his mother. She only lived across the playground, so she was there immediately. She drove him to the nearest hospital, 45 miles away.

After school I went directly to the hospital and stayed with his mother until midnight, because she had no family nearby. On the way to surgery, the boy came by the waiting room where we were. As he was rolled past me, he reached for my hand and told me he loved me. Wow! He came through the surgery great and was sent home the next day. After Christmas break he came back as chipper as ever.

One day, the thing we all fear happened. The boy's mother came into my classroom, with all 34 of my students present. She announced she was suing me. Coincidentally, or maybe not so coincidentally, our school had had a workshop at the beginning of the year on lawsuits. A legal representative from our state teacher's association had informed us that there were people who viewed teachers as an easy target. She told us that in the event someone threatened to sue us, we should not try to handle it ourselves, but should contact the association as soon as possible. So when this came up, I wasn't as naive as I might have otherwise been. When the woman came in my room that day, I was so put out with her that I gave her the name and number of the legal representative of the teacher's organization and the number of our superintendent and told her to call them. I was so angry I told her I had nothing else to say to her. I immediately contacted our superintendent and our state teacher's organization. The parent also contacted both.

I made a decision then and there that I wasn't going to let the situation get the best of me. At the time I thought to myself that she wasn't worth it. She wasn't worth losing my enthusiasm for teaching or my caring for my kids. That's what got me through it. The other teachers who are my basic realm of friends were also a great source of support.

I never heard anything else about being sued. The parent never mentioned it again. I don't know what events led to her decision not to sue me, but I was grateful nothing ever came of it. I hope I never come that close again; but if I do, I know I can live through it, and now I know there are people and organizations to support me."

Laurie Whitlock is one to whom others go for advice. But she is not afraid to admit that she, too, has fears.

"I'm afraid I turn kids off. I do everything I can not to, but kids are so accustomed to videos and new technology. I can't compete with the audio/video industry. I'm afraid sometimes that I discourage kids rather than encourage them. When I see kids not achieving, I do a lot of soul-searching. Is it me? Is it them?

If I discover that my fear is not valid (that my students are choosing not to achieve), then I fight the battle of not giving up. I look for new ways of presenting, trying to get into the kids' minds to find out what they are thinking so

I can relate. To demonstrate that sound is the result of the vibration of atoms and molecules, I've taken my class of seventh graders outside, had them stand an arm's length apart, and jump up and down, reflecting on how they moved in relation to the others next to them. When they move closer together and jump up and down, they 'see' a picture of sound traveling faster through solids than through gas.

"Worry never robs tomorrow of its sorrow; it only saps today of its strength."   A.J. Cronin

One time in chemistry when we were discussing ionization energy (the energy needed to take an electron away from an atom), I reached over and jerked a pen from a student's hand. She looked surprised as did the other students, but I explained the following: 1) I had removed an 'electron', which was relatively easy because she held it loosely (not having been prepared for my actions), and 2) it required some energy on my part to do so. Students remembered this demonstration, and several referred back to the example as one that helped them remember the concept.

The day I decide to give up, the day I want to quit, when I say this is it, that's the day a kid comes up and says, 'Golly, this is the best class I've ever had.'"

Different is Only Different

Our emotions can get us in trouble. This can happen when we compare ourselves to other teachers. When we go to conferences, workshops, or perhaps even the classroom next door, we hear many new and creative ideas used by other teachers. When we look at what others are doing, we can get discouraged and may feel we aren't doing enough. Most of us have a strong tendency to compare ourselves with others; we should use this to learn from others, realizing

Just as snowflakes differ, no two of us teach just alike. There's room for all of us.

that we, too, have unique strengths. It would help us to realize that what we are doing is just as new to other teachers as their ideas are to us.

Jan Bryan, a reading colleague of mine (Beth's), taught me the concept "different is only different" during a conversation about the creative styles and strategies we see in other teachers. Jan, who taught elementary school and reading for many years and is now a reading consultant, first learned about the concept as a young girl.

"I was a twirler. I was everything a 12-year-old in a much-too-short velvet uniform and tasseled boots could be. My twirling teacher, Ann, and I had been working together since I was nine. I idolized her.

I walked to the gym, knowing front-hand spins, figure eights, parade struts, and simple, yet precise solo routines. I was confident. Then I watched the 'faster, stronger, higher' twirlers try out before me. Tears flooded my face. My clammy palms could not hold a baton, much less twirl it. 'I

"Use what talents you have— the woods would be silent if no bird sang except those that sing best."   Unknown

can't beat these girls. They're better than me.' Those were the only words I could manage between sobs. 'You're not here to beat these girls. You're here to twirl. They're not better than you. They just know different stuff.'

I would love to report that I marched into that gym, twirled my heart out, and became the first seventh-grade twirler at Lincoln Junior High, but I must be honest. I didn't twirl that day. I just cried. Ann's words fell on deaf ears that day. But like any great teacher, Ann continues to teach me today. You're not here to beat anyone. You're here to do what you are capable of doing. Different is only different.

As a classroom teacher, I have echoed Ann's wisdom in many ways. In my second-grade classroom, I focused on cooperative learning each day. After recess, we would return to our classroom and tackle a story problem for math. My second graders worked in teams. Each team was to solve the problem and share their ideas with the entire class. In addition to social skills, I found that I had to teach my second graders to distinguish between 'different' and 'better.'

One of my favorite problems concerned a particularly slimy snail. It seems that this snail wanted to scale a ten-meter garden wall. Each day, our industrious friend climbed two meters. Each night, the slimy little fellow slipped back down one meter. At this rate, how many days will it take our snail to get to the top of the garden wall? (Of course what he would have done when he got there is of little concern at this point.) I encouraged my second graders to think about all the different ways they could solve the problem. This was a trick because they were all convinced that the snail would reach the top of the wall in ten days and saw no reason to work further. However, I pulled rank and insisted that each team give it a go. Some teams drew the wall and the snail. Some teams talked logically about the facts of the problem and then stated their conclusion. One team even developed a complex graph. The important thing is that each team employed different approaches to the same problem.

When it was time to share, I emphasized again and again that different approaches led to the same (correct) answer. Different is only different became an overriding theme in my second-grade classroom, in my teaching, and in my life.

During this same time, I taught across the hall from a phenomenal second-grade teacher. She was so organized. Her room was orderly and her students well mannered. In contrast, my classroom was a zoo. I was shocked to learn that this teacher felt inadequate compared to me. While her students were working through difficult phonic concepts, my students were writing about their community, misspelling even the most simple words (by the way, 'different is only different' does not apply to spelling). While her students were mastering math facts, mine were trying to get a snail up the garden wall. One afternoon, she looked into my classroom, saw bits of construction paper scattered everywhere, dictionaries lying open, first drafts waiting to be corrected. She said through frustration and tears, 'I'm a terrible teacher.'

I was dumbfounded. This remarkable teacher, this woman who had taught my own two children, looked at my 'different' classroom and felt inadequate. Once I found the courage to speak, I shared a gift that had been given to me many years ago. I said, 'Mary Jo, you are not here to compete with me, you are here to teach. I am not a better teacher than you. I just know different stuff. I'm so grateful to you for what my children have learned in your classroom. You have helped them master the basics of composition and calculation. These are concepts they use every day. You have shown them the beauty of an organized life. You can see what they must get at home! Mary Jo, different is only different.'"

High school English teacher Kimberlea Gray has learned some lessons during her tenure of teaching.

"Teaching and learning are individual. What works for one teacher or student does not always work for another. If a teacher cannot adapt to expectations from a particular school district or administration, it does not mean that he or she is a failure. I believe that each educator can find a district that is right for her. Some of us find our niche in the first school in which we teach, while others must search. I have seen too many good first-year teachers quit because they felt or were told that they were incompetent because they did not agree or practice the teaching techniques viewed as acceptable by that district.

"Each one of us is a unique event in the universe."
Juan Mascaro

In addition, good teaching takes time. I am a different teacher today than I was two years, five years, ten years, or twelve years ago. If I am not, then I need to look at another profession. I hope I will continue to grow and improve with age, like a good wine."

Fuel for the Fire
IDEAS TO INCORPORATE

- Make laughter a regular part of your day. Reflect back on things that have made you laugh in the past. Look for opportunities around you to laugh. Let students who use their good humor appropriately know that you value their wit.

- Learn to laugh at yourself. When you make a mistake, find something in it to smile about. You might even be bold enough to make a joke. Your students probably caught the error anyway, and they will appreciate seeing you admit that you are a real person.

- Read stories to your class that have a humorous tone. Even older students enjoy being read to upon occasion. Lots of literature is available with good, clean humor such as *The True Story of the Three Little Pigs* by Jon Scieszka for lower elementary students; *There's a Boy in the Girls' Bathroom* by Louis Sacher for upper elementary; "Charles" by Shirley Jackson, and *Summer of the Monkeys* by Wilson Rawls for middle school students; and "Ransom of Red Chief" by O Henry for high schoolers.

- Display posters or comic strips that make their point with a bit of levity.

- Read jokes to your class. Begin the first day of school with a joke that will ease the students' minds, and let them see that you are not afraid of laughter in the classroom.

- Take inventory. What fears are haunting you? Are you worrying about the same things consistently? Identify these fears. Decide whether your fears are valid.

- If you have valid fears, take specific steps to deal with them. Write on a piece of paper things you can do. This will help you to see some options. Do not be afraid to get advice from wise counsel. It is necessary to confront your fears and not to stuff them down.
- Write down the fears that you hold on to that are not valid fears. Read the list carefully. Burn the list. Every time that fear comes back to you, remember that you got rid of it.
- If you find yourself getting discouraged because you feel other teachers seem to be doing more than you are, take a good look at the ideas you use in your classroom that are original to you.
- Set up a classroom atmosphere that is not competitive. Teach your students the importance of valuing what they do.

Just for the Preservice Teacher

- Make a list of good, clean jokes you can share with your future classes. Student teacher Renee Cook writes jokes on index cards and occasionally passes them out to students to read to the class.
- Make a list of things you are nervous about concerning being a teacher. Share your list with a teacher or one of your professors. Chances are they will help you see that your fears are normal.

PART THREE

KEEP THE LIGHT SHINING

TURN CHALLENGES INTO OPPORTUNITES

As educators, we have been trained to focus on the student. We are told to define his needs, identify her problems, discern the educational strategies we can use to benefit him most. While of course it is important that we focus on our students, we have learned that as we teach, we need to look at ourselves as well. If we are enjoying what we do and are excited about a subject, idea, or concept, we will be much more successful at generating enthusiasm among our students. Dale Carnegie, who learned from successful leaders in the field of business, quoted a man as saying, "A man rarely succeeds at anything unless he has fun doing it. I have known men who succeeded because they had a rip-roaring good time conducting their business. Later, I saw those men begin to work at the job. It grew dull. They lost all joy in it, and they failed." We as teachers can learn a great deal from this man's observations. When we are having a good time, when we make teaching meaningful for us, we will be successful, fulfilled teachers.

Before takeoff on an airplane, one of the instructions that flight attendants give to parents in case of an emergency is to put on their own air masks before their children's. If parents pass out from lack of oxygen, they cannot help their children. The same can be said for teachers. If we become burned out because of a lack of passion, we will not be as effective in helping our students. We need to be aware of what makes teaching meaningful for us because as we make it work for us, it will work for our students as well.

Make it Meaningful for You

As you make your teaching meaningful for you, your students will also benefit.

No one can change the environment in our classrooms but us. It is our responsibility to make it what we want it to be. If we have become complacent in our teaching, then we need to ask ourselves, "What can I do today that will make this a meaningful and fulfilling day?" Instead of focusing only on meeting curricular objectives and doing paperwork, we can change our perspective by changing our question. How can we teach what we need to teach in ways that will be interesting and relevant to us? We can make teaching more meaningful by adding our own personalities, styles, and interests to what we do. Teaching is like a good marriage; you don't have a happy marriage when only one person is happy, and you don't have a successful classroom when only the teacher or only the students are happy.

It has been said that the best thing a father can do for his children is to love their mother and vice versa. The same can be said for a classroom. The best thing we as teachers can do for our students is to enjoy being teachers and to find ways to make teaching meaningful for us. That can mean a variety of things for different teachers. Some bring in their own interests, others use their creativity. For Laurie Whitlock, making it meaningful has yet another twist.

"My husband asks me why after so many years of teaching I still spend so much time grading papers and planning lessons. I explain to him it is because I want to give my students the best education possible. After I had kids, I looked at my teaching from a different perspective.

The only way I can expect my own children to get a good education is for me to work to provide the same for other people's children. This makes teaching more meaningful to me."

Incorporating Your Own Interests

After 20 years of teaching, the last 11 at the same school, I (Ginny) was feeling some burnout. Teaching the same subject class after class, day after day was wearing on me. Not that I didn't try different things or new approaches, but I just felt, well . . . stagnant. I had a student

Bringing your own interests into your classroom will add meaning to your teaching.

teacher the first quarter that year, and while I had some extra time I began reading the book *In the Middle* by Nancie Atwell. It was exciting to read about the reading/writing workshop she had developed. Atwell created a classroom environment where students were motivated to read and write. She guided her students as they worked on individual goals. I spent hours studying, planning, organizing, and dreaming about how I could set up this same atmosphere in my classroom.

By the time my student teacher had finished his block, I was ready. I introduced the concept. It would be a new experience to use textbooks only as resources and completely revise my grading system. Setting goals, conferencing with the teacher and other students, completing reading logs, going public with writing pieces—we were breaking new ground, at least in our territory. We jumped in with both feet.

Class time was divided into reading days and writing days. On reading days, students reported to me the books they were presently reading and I gave them time to read in class. Once a week they were required to correspond through a letter in a literature log about their reading. I responded to their letters, adding comments about my own reading. Writing days were spent working on pieces they initiated. I conferenced with them as they progressed, and they also conferred with their peers. Much time was spent on the revision and editing of their pieces. At the beginning of each class period I presented brief mini-lessons relating to some skill or factual information.

> "Do what intrigues you, explore what interests you; think mystery, not mastery."
> Julia Cameron in *The Artist's Way*

This approach was one of the best teaching experiences I have had. Students read voraciously and were eager to work on their writing pieces. The student evaluations at the end of the year verified that I had made the right decision. Students who admitted they had never finished a book were excited to discover that reading is fun. It thrilled me to be asked by those I would have next year if I would please do reading/writing workshop again. And, as an extra bonus, our state achievement test results were significantly higher.

Sometimes, when you get in a rut, you force your students to be in one, too. I became excited about something, and that energy transferred to my students. I agree with Perrone (1991), who said that "teachers need opportunities to reflect on their learning, on how they first came to the interests they possess and how to revitalize those interests." Incorporating my interests and learning new techniques certainly did revitalize my teaching and my attitude.

Veteran teacher Schyrlet Cameron recently received the 1997 Presidential Award for Excellence in Science and Mathematics Teaching. She likes projects and enjoys writing grants (she's written 13), not only because they benefit her students but also because it keeps teaching interesting for her.

"I always have a lot of projects going all the time, both at school and at home. I have been that way all my life. At school I may have five or six projects going. And the kids have projects too. We recently started a mail system in our school, and my students named our room 'Project Plaza.' I thought that was so funny. I do these projects for the kids, but I love them.

The project I was working on when I won the Presidential Award was one I had written a grant for. It was called 'The Case of the Missing Millionaire.' The students were given information about a crime that had been committed. The classroom was cleared and the students reenacted the crime scene. The local sheriff came to talk to the 'suspects.' The students had to study the facts to solve the case. We even visited the county courthouse and met with the circuit judge. Back at school we reenacted the court case, videotaping the whole thing. We even had jurors who made the verdict. The students and I both had a ball with this. As soon as I finish one project like this, I have another one ready to go.

These projects give me something to think about. I can be driving down the road, and I will be thinking about my next project. I need to be creating and doing. I'm not the kind of person who can sit home and watch TV. I'm not involved in it. As a teacher, I'm right there, actively involved. And I am trying to get the kids involved with me. I tell them anything is possible. I tell them to let their minds wander. If they want to do a project, I tell them to think of the wildest thing they could do. I want them to do anything other than writing a report. That was so boring for me as a student. And reading their reports is boring for me as a teacher. But with projects I learn so much.

One of the things I get out of writing grants is the personal feeling of knowing that I can do it. It takes me a long time to write a grant. I am a terrible writer. I struggle with every word. I see it as a self-help thing. They are my projects. I get a great sense of accomplishment when I complete one. If a grant is not accepted, I don't view it as a setback or a failure. When that happens, I read the reviews and suggestions, rewrite it, and submit it the next year.

Last year one of the kids said, 'Mrs. Cameron, you must really love us a lot to write these grants for us so we get to do so many neat things.'

And I said, 'I really do. I do this because I want you to learn and the best way to do that is if you are having fun.'"

Becky Loyd, first-grade teacher, says she gets "fired up" by using her skills and talents to help others.

"I've been teaching now for seven years and one of the things I've recently found to be motivating is helping a younger teacher. A friend of mine recently started teaching. She began in the middle of the year and entered a rather difficult situation. I offered to help her get organized, and we began to work together on her activities and lessons plans. Not only did the time we spend together benefit her but it encouraged me to open my mind and create new ideas. When she asked for advice and I began sharing with her, suddenly it hit me, 'Hey, that would solve my own problem!' For example, she was having trouble with time management. I suggested that she develop a schedule for herself. Then I realized I was stressed out too because that year, due to overcrowding, our students had art and music in our classrooms, which left us teachers without full access to our rooms during those planning periods. Why hadn't I thought before to schedule my own tasks for a particular time? On Mondays when I had planning time during recess, I could clean off my desk, or on Wednesday when I was able to be in my room I could work on bulletin boards, and so on. Then on the days I was not able to work in my room, I could plan to do things that could be done elsewhere such as grading papers.

"You give but little when you give of your possessions. It is when you give of yourself that you truly give." Kahlil Gibran

I realize we get into 'ruts' and do the same things year after year because they are familiar and effective. But as I began to reopen my mind and create, I became excited and motivated again. My time with the younger teacher has become a two-way discussion of what we are preparing to do each week. We start with skeleton ideas, and the brainstorming brings all kinds of specifics. I encourage everyone to find a person with whom to collaborate. It's an extremely motivating experience.

Something else that excites me is writing grants. A good friend and I collaborated in writing four grants two years ago, on both the local and state levels. Each one was theme oriented. For example, one was called Spring Surprise and the theme was butterflies.

The money we got allowed us to purchase items that we wouldn't otherwise be able to get. We were able to use the butterfly theme in every area of study by using a tent, books, butterfly net, math materials, craft supplies, videos on butterflies, authors of the books, etc. With another grant we purchased a grow light. We also tie that in with every unit. When we study Black history, we grow cotton or peanuts. When we are in the butterfly unit we grow marigolds and spring flowers.

Collaborating with other teachers and helping someone else rejuvenates and adds that beginning 'freshness' back to our teaching. Isn't it wonderful how helping someone else turns into a blessing for us?"

Jill Campbell, who has taught kindergarten for over 15 years, has found that sharing her personal self in her classroom makes school more rewarding for both her and her students.

"I like to let my students see a little bit of myself so they can get to know me. One way I do this is by bringing in personal things. For example, I like penguins, so I have pictures of them around the room as well as knick-knacks such as my penguin treat jar. When we learn the letter 'P,' I tell them my most favorite animal in the whole wide world is a penguin. Then they associate the letter 'P' with penguins. I use part of who I am to help them learn.

Since they all know I like penguins, they look for things with penguins to give to me. They often bring me little penguin gifts they have found while on trips with their families. They like to add to my collection. It makes them feel good to see I value their gifts."

June Brown spent years teaching children how to read, and now she teaches prospective teachers how to teach children to read. Because reading is such a passion for her, she thoroughly enjoys passing on her love of reading to others.

"If teachers are excited about reading and writing, their students probably will 'catch' that enthusiasm because it is contagious. Because I absolutely love to read and write, my students begin to anticipate the thrill of literature as well. This enthusiasm is essential whether you are teaching children or adults.

I like to keep current regarding the numerous children's books published each year. The excitement I feel over sharing old literary friends and finding new treasures keeps me authentic, interested, and, hopefully, interesting as well. For if I am not having fun teaching, my students are probably not having fun learning either. So, the first rule for me is Keep It Fun!

I have found that elementary education majors still love to be read to. The top 'turn-on' to inspire others to read is still reading aloud. Therefore, I begin the semester reading to my students and continue throughout the weeks of class, introducing them to numerous quality children's books and authors. Their eyes sparkle with anticipation each time I take a new book to class. I also allow them to buy books at discounted prices through children's book clubs. There is a kind of magic that occurs when you put excellent books in the hands of children and adults. Just as my elementary students used to do, my college students get excited when they see me carrying their books from the book clubs. They love to examine and share their new purchases with their classmates.

> "If you follow a path that interests you—hopefully with a passion—and if you bring to it a sense of your own worth . . . and do not make success or failure the criteria by which you live, chances are you will be a person worthy of your own respect." Neil Simon

To continue to spark their imagination, I introduce numerous ways to create literature response activities centered around specific books. For example, we read the poem, 'If I Were in Charge of the World' by Judith Viorst, and then create our own parallel class poems from their perspective as college students in charge of the university. Then I share my version about stamping out dyslexia from the viewpoint of a reading professor and have my students create illustrations for a class book. At first they tell me they cannot draw but eventually seem delighted in the outcome of our work. I know the activities have been successful because students frequently repeat them with children in their practicums.

Another literature response idea I have found that motivates students of all ages is to combine food with books. We nibble on fish crackers while creating an interdisciplinary unit using *The Magic School Bus on the Ocean Floor* (Cole, 1992). Art is also a good motivator. We make posters to serve as book commercials. We use artwork to illustrate important story elements or comprehension strategies. We create pop-up, accordion, flap, and numerous other shape books. We'll do anything to make reading come alive for students and to make reading fun."

Teaching as a Creative Outlet

One of the great things about teaching is that you have the freedom to be as creative as your heart desires. Having a creative outlet in which you can express your aesthetic side through art, music, drama, poetry, or by letting your imaginative mind flow with new ideas can be a wonderful source of pleasure and inspiration. I (Beth) found a journal from high school in which I had written, "I feel like I have all this creative energy inside me and have nothing to do with it." Maybe that is why I fell in love with teaching, and definitely why I chose to begin my teaching career in the elementary

> Creating learning experiences for your students can also serve as a creative outlet for you.

classroom. I am the kind of person who is, as the saying goes, "a jack of all trades, master of none." There are many things I enjoy—art, music, history, reading. Elementary teachers teach every subject, so I thought that would be a perfect place for me to explore and further develop my interests in every discipline.

To me, being a teacher is a gift. Where else could I get paid to draw pictures and color them with magic markers or stand in front of 30 people and break into song just because the mood strikes me, or tell jokes and make people laugh? Finally, I have what I always dreamed of: I have an outlet for all the creative energy that is bursting to get out. And to top that, I have a room full of students who have the same needs to create as I do.

When we look at teaching in this light, when we view school as a place to do what we love with people we enjoy, it becomes more than a job. Teaching is an extension of who we are. Flossie Parke, a former elementary teacher who taught for 31 years, talks about how she enjoyed creating meaningful learning activities so much that she continues to look for ways to create even though she is retired.

"I wanted my classroom filled with creative activities that make children want to learn. I spent endless hours of my own time and money looking for and buying things such as little animals for every letter of the alphabet or at Halloween, masks for every vowel sound. I do not like to walk into a classroom that is drab, so I wanted mine to be bright and cheery. I did it for the students, but I did it for me too. Now that I am retired I have been invited to visit several classrooms to read to the children. My favorite book to read is *Aunt Flossie's Hats: And Crab Cakes Later* by Elizabeth Fitzgerald Howard because my name is in it. When your name is Flossie you don't see your name in many books or stories. On the back cover of the book the author states that the story is based on her Aunt Flossie Wright who was a schoolteacher. My maiden name was Wright, and I was a teacher also. When I was first invited to read to children at school, I thought it would be fun to find hats to match Aunt Flossie's hats. My 93-year-old Aunt Sally gave me an old hat box, a mink hat, and a black hat, all similar to those in the book. I continued collecting hat boxes and hats until I had all of the important hats in the story, including a straw hat with pink and yellow flowers with a green velvet ribbon, just like Aunt Flossie's favorite Sunday hat. As I read Aunt Flossie's memory stories I put on the hat from that story. The children laugh merrily as I put on the same hats as those in the book.

"Imagination is more important than knowledge."
Albert Einstein

After reading at a particular school, a teacher asked me if I would come read the book at a senior citizen's home. The elderly women enjoyed seeing the old hats and hearing the stories as much, if not more, than the children. A highlight for the schoolchildren and the senior citizens is when I give each of them a paper hat decorated as Aunt Flossie's favorite hat, with a magnet for their refrigerator. I enjoy the challenge of finding new and different ways of representing a story in order to make reading a meaningful experience.

These types of activities make children want to read, and for me, they kept me eager for the school day to begin. While it is true they required a lot of time and effort on my part, I did not see them as a chore; it was more like a hobby that gave me a great deal of satisfaction. That's why, even though I am retired from teaching, I still read to schoolchildren, make bulletin boards for my church, make teaching things for my daughter who is a teacher, and why I still buy coloring books when they are on sale."

Lori Elliott feels that she could not survive without teaching because it provides her with an outlet to create.

"I love coming up with ideas to use in my classroom. I have to have these creative outlets. I would wither and die if I couldn't do this. I have to let my thinking flow. Teaching allows me the freedom to be as creative as I want to be.

I love to plan themes. In my room we go from one theme to another. Within that theme I incorporate every subject matter. It has become like a game for me. It's like, let me see how many ways I can talk about chocolate. We make bar graphs, line graphs, and pie graphs using M&M's; we read *Willy Wonka and the Chocolate Factory;* we write letters to the Hershey company; we study the ingredients for chocolate and learn about importing and exporting of goods; we study advertising and write and videotape commercials; we weigh and measure chocolate; we figure calories and how much energy it takes to work off those calories; we learn about nutrition; we conduct interviews and collect data about how much chocolate people eat and their favorite kinds; we read, research, and learn everything there is to know about chocolate such as when it was invented and where and how it is made; and, of course, we eat chocolate.

Each of my themes usually lasts about three weeks. I do most of my planning for my themes in the summer so when school starts I am ready to go. You'd think that once I had my themes ready for one year, I'd be all set and wouldn't have to plan anymore. But not with me. Once I've done the theme I'm ready to start thinking of another one. When I see something that goes with a theme I am teaching, or an outfit that matches my theme, I just have to have it. (My students call me Ms. Frizzle from the Magic School Bus series because I always have an outfit to go with my themes.)

Yes, I do spend a lot of my own money. My husband says I don't make any money because I spend it all on school. But I spend it because I want to, not because I have to. Buying things for my classroom is fun for me. It's like a hobby—it's how I enjoy spending my time and my money. In teaching, you get what you give.'

The second graders in Amy Billings's class reap the benefits of her creative energy.

"Little did I know that years of singing, dancing, and acting in high school would be some of my greatest tools when it came to teaching second graders. Remembering how much I hated the 'lights off' trick that my primary teachers used when they wanted everyone's attention, I have instead come up with numerous songs, both sung and played on a little xylophone that I keep in my room, to let my class know I need for them to listen. One of the things I love about teaching young children is that they will respond to my dramatic craziness. Last week when I wanted them to pick everything up off of the floor, I remembered the words to an old cheer from high school. I 'revised' it on the spot, and started to chant, 'N-O-T-H-I-N-G on the floor's what I should see. Nothing, absolutely nothing!' In no time the kids were chanting with me and picking up all the clutter off the floor! Another simple song I made up says, 'Stop and look. Turn and hear. Mrs. Billings needs listening ears.' Of course I spend time teaching my class what I expect when I use these 'signals' as I call them, but I have found it is so much more pleasant for me (and I suppose for them too) to be able to burst into song when I want their attention rather than yell, turn off lights, or say, 'boys and girls' a hundred times a day.

My love of music is used in other ways in my classroom that help with teaching particular concepts and just add fun and variety to my/our day. I have songs to help students remember things such as the names of the continents, oceans, the 50 states, the seasons of the year, months, days of the week, information about George Washington, Martin Luther King, Jr., and the story of the Titanic. Each day during our opening exercises I read to my class from a little book called *Do You Know What Day Tomorrow Is?* by Lee Bennett Hopkins. One day I was reading about John Philip Sousa and I asked my class if anyone knew why he was famous. They didn't, so I explained that he was

> "It is the supreme art of the teacher to awaken joy in creative expression and knowledge."
> Albert Einstein

a famous musician who wrote marches for bands. With that, an idea popped into my head, and soon the whole class was marching around the room while I loudly hummed one of his marches. The kids were laughing and following me as we marched to my rendition of the 'Stars and Stripes Forever.'

It is my hope that, at the very least, the children in my class will never be bored and may remember something about Sousa through marching that just reading about him wouldn't have accomplished. The day I read about Oklahoma becoming a state, I began to sing the theme song from the musical 'Oklahoma.' My class wanted to learn it too.

I love to be spontaneous, and I believe if the children have a certain element of wonder about what I may do next, it keeps them attentive and hopefully learning more. One day while teaching a lesson about the correct formation of the numeral '8' I looked up at my chart only to discover that the '8' was upside down. It was up high on the wall, so without missing a beat, I continued to talk as I stepped on a chair and then on a desk and turned the numeral over. When I looked back at the class, they all had a look of disbelief on their faces. I guess they were surprised I would/could stand on a desk. Another day when teaching a lesson I spied a toy microphone lying in the chalk tray. I picked it up and began to pretend I was a game-show host, and as I asked questions I would go up to the child who was answering and let him/her talk into the microphone. Needless to say, everyone wanted a turn to answer a question that day.

One of my favorite things about being a teacher is that it allows me to be creative. I spend hours thinking about how I will decorate my classroom door for the beginning of each school year. For me, it's almost a game I play with myself to see if I can come up with something better than the year before. This year I covered my door with royal blue paper, made a fish border all the way around it, and cut out letters that said, 'We're hooked on learning in second grade.' I made individual fish for each student, complete with a big sequin for the eye, glitter on the tail, and the child's name, and then made fishing rods out of dowel rods with white yarn for the line. At the end of each fishing line was a book made out of different colored construction paper with the names of subjects like math, reading, spelling, writing, science, and social studies. I had a great time designing it and watching it take shape as I placed each piece on the door. Some people think I'm nuts to spend the time and energy on a door, but to me it is a child's first impression of what life in my room will be like and I want them to want to come into my room and see what it's all about.

Maybe because I have had my share of 'serious' teachers, my silliness is my own private way of rebelling against all that. Maybe it's because I believe there is so much to be learned that I'll do anything I can to make that learning more fun, more engaging, and more exciting. Or, maybe I'm just a big kid at heart and I love to laugh, enjoy myself, and be silly. Whatever the reason(s), teaching is the profession that allows me to create, play, and be dramatic on my own little stage in the second grade. At the very least my students learn a lot of songs, but more importantly, I hope they leave my classroom with the sense that learning new things can be incredibly fun. It certainly is fun for me!"

Learning from Your Students

Ralph Waldo Emerson said, "Every man I meet is my superior in some way. In that, I learn of him." It has been said that we are all teachers and we are all students. As teachers, it would behoove us to listen carefully to these two bits of wisdom. One way we can make teaching more meaningful for us is to allow ourselves to become learners with and from our students.

"You have as much to learn from children as you have to teach them." Barbara DeAngelis in *Real Moments*

I (Beth) once heard a definition of equality that has always stayed in my mind. I heard that every person in our lives has as much to offer us as we have to offer him. The more I have thought about this and put it to the test in my thinking and experiences, the more true it seems to be. Often as teachers we view ourselves as the givers. We are there to give to our students. But if this theory of equality is true, then our students are there as much for us as we are there for them; we will receive as well as give. It is a beautiful thing, but we may not realize it unless we look for it. Regie Routman, one of my favorite educational authors, who has written books such as *Invitations* and *Transitions*, describes a classroom she visited as a "a joyful, collaborative community where the teacher and learners supported and learned from each other." When we view ourselves as co-learners with our students, magical things can happen in our classrooms.

This is true from the lower elementary level all the way to college. Children have a way of expressing profound thoughts in their innocence. At times, we adults are left dumbfounded by their perceptions.

My (Ginny's) mother, a teacher for many years, often told a story as I was growing up about something that happened in the junior high school in which she taught. She was standing on hall duty as students changed classes when a young girl dashed down the hall. She told the girl to slow down, which she did long enough to reply, "Okay, Mrs. Bartley." Then she resumed her interrupted speed. In a short time, my mother says, the girl reappeared at her side. "I'm sorry I called you Mrs. Bartley. It's just that you two look so much alike." Then she took off again. The people surrounding my mother grinned; some even laughed aloud. You see, Mrs. Bartley was 20 years older than my mom; she was tall, and she was black. My mother is quite short and white. Mama always said that she guessed the girl looked inside and knew that she and Mrs. Bartley were alike. They both cared. That little girl has taught many of us adults a lesson through that incident, and she never even knew it.

As teachers, we will be more genuine and approachable to our students if they see that we respect them for the knowledge they have. It may not be easy to admit that a first grader knows more than we do, but there are times when that may very well be the case.

Susan Wilson has had a variety of experiences with elementary students. She worked as an aid in a special services classroom, substituted for a variety of age groups, and has taught in first-, second-, and third-grade classrooms. She recalls one of many incidents when her students were the teachers and she was the student.

"While teaching a first-grade class in Winter Harbor, Maine, a lesson on consonants, I had the students color a paper that was a part of the lesson. I noticed one of the children coloring a lobster green. I said to her, 'Lobsters are red, not green.' She turned to me and said, 'They're only red after they are cooked.' You see, I had grown up in South Dakota and had never seen a lobster, much less known their natural color. That was a day the teacher learned a good lesson from her student."

Jill Campbell has learned that you can even learn from kindergartners.

"One of the skills we work on in kindergarten is, 'Which one of these items does not belong?' I show the students three or four objects and they have to pick which one does not belong with the others. Recently I showed the kids the following four objects: a magic marker, a pen, a bottle of glue, and a pencil. Which one doesn't belong? The glue, right? Well, that's what I thought, but one of my students shouted out, 'The pencil!' Rather than telling her she was wrong, I asked her why she thought it was the pencil to get her to think about what she had said so she could figure out for herself why she was wrong. She surprised me when she said, 'The pencil is the only one without a lid.' Her thinking was beyond mine.

"Life is like playing a violin solo in public and learning the instrument as one goes on."
Samuel Butler

I learned my lesson from that experience. When I later tested the children on the concept, if a student missed one, I called that student to my desk to ask for an explanation of the answer. One boy missed this one: a green dinosaur, a yellow car, and a green ball. He had answered green dinosaur instead of yellow car. His explanation: 'because the car and the ball both roll.' There again, a five-year-old thought of something I hadn't."

Learning is Forever

We love to learn. To us, learning is not just something we do at school; learning takes place in our everyday lives, or as an old Chinese saying goes, in our chopping wood and carrying water. We learn as we tend our gardens, shop at the mall, go to parties, or read the newspaper. All of life is a learning process. Whether we are discovering better ways of handling relationships, new ways of solving problems, or a more effective way of doing our job, we are learning something. Part of our job as teachers is to show our students how we learn in all situations. In their book *Content Area Reading*, Vacca and Vacca discuss a teaching strategy called "think-alouds." With this strategy, teachers talk about or think aloud their own thinking, reasoning, and learning processes. For example, if you are reading aloud to your students and you come to an unknown word, stop and say something like, "I don't remember seeing this word before. I am not sure what it means, but by using context clues, or by looking at the other words around it, I think it means . . ." Then ask a student to look it up in the dictionary to see if your guess was correct. You are demonstrating to your students what you do when you come to an unknown word. Then hopefully when they are reading and come to a word they don't know, they will remember what to do.

> "By learning you will teach; by teaching you will learn."
> Latin proverb

By teaching our students how to ask questions, how to find their own answers, and by watching us do the same, we are teaching them how to become lifelong learners. It is important that we are active members in the learning process in our classrooms. We need to let our students see that we are learning with them, that learning is not just something that happens in school, that learning is forever, and that part of the fun of living is in learning. We are not effectively teaching if we are not creating opportunities for our own learning.

Teachers are often seen as the "experts," expected to know all the answers. I (Ginny) remember that in my first year of teaching, I was responsible for working with a very difficult, emotionally disturbed second grader. His father would come to me for advice, saying, "You just tell me what to do. You're the expert!" Those of us who teach know the truth—that we are a long way from knowing all the answers. But, there is a difference in realizing we don't know everything and in having the desire to continue learning. Teachers should never be satisfied that they have learned enough. We teachers are in the business of igniting in our students that excitement of learning. If we are not involved in the process ourselves, our own light is dimmed.

Bob Brady shares some of his own philosophy about learning.

"One reason we become teachers is because we like learning. I have some flexibility in what I teach and how I teach it. I might make a lesson on a theme about something I've not learned or perhaps something I want to learn more about. I make it an excuse for learning. For example, this year my students were required to memorize a poem by Goethe, the great German poet. I used this opportunity to do some personal research on his life. I tried to connect this guy with what my students were learning in eleventh- and twelfth-grade history and literature. I learned a lot in doing this, and some of my students got involved in researching Goethe as well. I have done the same with Martin Luther. On the 450th anniversary of his death, I created a unit. Students got involved in the story of Luther's life and his contributions, and together we learned a great deal about him. We discussed how this study was an appropriate one for our German class. Luther's translation of the Bible in German coincided with the country's more extensive use of the printing press; through this, a standard for the German language was created.

"I was still learning when I taught my last class."
Claude M. Fuess, after forty years of teaching.

I have found that you have to look for opportunities to keep learning for your own self-satisfaction. Just because you have a credential doesn't mean that you've stopped learning."

Elementary teacher Lori Elliott has a fresh outlook on new trends in education.

"I overheard a teacher at a conference say, 'Some teachers say that trends in education run in cycles so they quit paying attention to them, but I learn something each time they come around.' I really liked that. I am always on the lookout for good ideas, and I feel like I can learn from anyone or anything. I am constantly learning. I learn more and more that you never arrive. The more I learn, the more I want to learn. The more I learn, the more I want to change and get better.

I've had people ask me how I know the material I teach with my units. I just tell them I am researching the information right along with my students. When I tell my kids that we are going to learn about what it was like to be a cowboy in the Old West, I mean literally *we* are going to learn about it. We go to the library together; we check out books; we get on the Internet; we read the encyclopedias. It's that constant learning that I love about teaching. I keep adding new themes to my curriculum because I want to be learning new things."

Learning new things is what keeps teacher Jana Loge going. She used to teach elementary school; now she teaches teachers throughout her state about how to improve assessment in their classrooms.

"I love teaching teachers about assessment because I am continuing to learn more about it every day. There is so much going on in the field with assessment right now that I could read a new article every day and not keep up. It's great!

I also learn a lot from teachers who are out there putting into practice these new techniques. I am seeing portfolios and rubrics that help teachers and students alike evaluate what is going on the classroom. I am seeing teachers and students learn to value what they know and what they can do. I have to be learning something new all the time or I think I'll lose my mind."

Veteran college teacher Genny Cramer explains that continued learning is what makes teaching so fulfilling for her even after years in the classroom.

"In the 25-plus years I have been teaching, I find I have to keep reaching out to learn and try new ideas or I begin to get stale, quit enjoying myself, and quit learning. Almost immediately my classes and my students also begin to get stale, quit enjoying themselves, and quit learning. I found for me the adage that the teacher is the most important learner in the room has certainly been true.

My first year of teaching was quite rocky. I was given a temporary certification and was hired to teach in a one-room country school with 21 students. I was so deadly serious in that year and so isolated. I had no colleagues to talk to and no time available in which to do it. I used to say I would have quit if the county courthouse, which handled resignations, had ever been open when I wasn't teaching.

In my second and third years, I taught a fourth-grade classroom in a progressive system in Colorado in which staff development was an important tool used with teachers. The turnaround for me was extraordinary. Learning from others and using that learning in the class became essential to me and still is.

Professional development keeps me growing, learning, and enjoying. Since that time, involvement in voluntary professional development has been a regular part of my teaching life. I learn about meetings, whether short-term or long-term, going on in our area and try to get permission to attend. Although I give presentations now, I much prefer to be a learner being exposed to others' ideas. I also try to be generous in my judgments. If I find I'm already familiar with the ideas presented, I try to look at it as indicative that I'm still aware of supported trends rather than thinking it a waste of time.

"If we do not have the desire to learn, we probably do not have the desire to teach."
Robert Evans, High School Science Teacher

I go to the local meetings of our International Reading Association (IRA). I am also active within my local council and in our local National Council of Teachers of English (NCTE) affiliate, which meets twice annually. Phi Delta Kappa, the Association for Curriculum and Development, and other groups are often available in particular local areas. State meetings of IRA and NCTE are usually close enough to attend as are State Department of Education meetings. Local association meetings are free to attend in our area as are all other councils I know about.

With professional development, I also like to use the advice of Joseph Campbell, the noted mythologist, to 'Follow your bliss.' I go to sessions or meetings that attract my attention and interest, as do most of the professionals I know. I've also found I need to incorporate ideas right away, or I can quickly forget them; they get buried in my stack of good ideas. So when I felt I needed help with comprehension, I read articles and attended conference sessions concerned with strategies to help. I watched Dorsey Hammond and Andree Bayliss model a Directed Reading-Thinking Activity, went back to my students and tried it out that week, and continue to use it regularly. When I attended an all-day workshop on teacher study groups, I tried to start one within two weeks. It took about eight months before I was part of a teacher study group that worked well. That group continues currently and has been the source of many good teaching ideas, collaborative writing projects, and has empowered professional development for me and the other members of the group. Our group has since written a Phi Delta Kappan Fastback on teacher study groups.

One of the professional development models that has interested me greatly is that of career stages suggested by Burke, Fessler, and Christensen, in a 1984 Phi Delta Kappan Fastback entitled *Teacher Career Stage: Implications for Staff Development,* which suggests that in the second half of many careers teachers begin to experience career frustrations, stagnation, and career wind-down, or what many of us would call burnout, as they lose their enthusiasm for teaching. The authors emphasize that staff development can help change this cycle. It has also been my experience in observing outstanding teachers that many good teachers continue to learn and grow, often using professional development, whether volunteer, planned, or otherwise. I know many exciting and excited teachers within months of retiring who are able to stay alive professionally by looking at new ideas, especially those they enjoy. It certainly has made a difference for me."

Making the Pieces Fit

Teaching involves many facets which, when pieced together, create a fascinating picture. One of the skills involved in teaching is that of taking the innumerable pieces and making them fit. My (Ginny's) family has a tradition at Christmas that has become a favorite. I find an interesting jigsaw puzzle early in the season. It must be just the right one, one everyone will enjoy. We keep it in the box until we have finished our holiday decorating, and then I get it out. *When the puzzle pieces have a tight fit, our lives are much easier.*
Dumping the pieces out on a card table or on the big dining room table, we begin to sort. Each piece is grouped by color or contrast and placed in its own area. As family members pass by on their way to some task, they stop for a minute. Often they tarry longer than anticipated as another person joins. Soon we are pulling chairs, crossing hands, looking for just the right piece, and every now and then we'll hear, "Got one!" Throughout the season, company will come and go, and many different hands will join in putting the puzzle together.

Teaching is a lot like a jigsaw puzzle. The big picture is laid out in front of you as you remember your background in education or as you prepare for your own teaching vocation. You know what the final product should look like, but the pieces aren't together. Many hands and much time are needed to make the pieces fit. It takes a lot of effort, including some elbow grease. Trial and error. A little bit of luck. But mostly it takes a person who just fits right in the middle of the puzzle, a person who is a part of the puzzle. In our interviews with teachers from all over the country, we frequently heard comments like, "It's my mission," "It's a calling," "Teaching is who I am," "I was born to teach." Those teachers are the ones who seem to be a ready-made part of the puzzle. They were cut out to fit. That's not to say that there aren't rough edges that need to be sanded or pieces that need to be trimmed, but they just seem to be made for teaching.

Dianne Renkoski says that teaching matches her personality to a tee.

"I think one of the reasons I like teaching so much, and why it seems to come so naturally to me, is because the skills necessary for teaching closely match my personality characteristics. I took a personality test once that showed I have the following personality traits: artistic, organized, list maker, likes to see the success of others, sets high standards for self and others, and is creative. I looked at that list and thought, 'No wonder I like teaching so much; these are the characteristics of a teacher.'

Many of the things that are part of teachers' jobs are things I would enjoy as a hobby. For example, I know some teachers don't enjoy making bulletin boards, but I think they are fun to design. I like to make 3-D bulletin boards like the one I made when we studied Mexico. I had traveled to Mexico and collected things I could use in my classes. A real sombrero was the center-piece of the bulletin board, surrounded by a newspaper, puppets, and other items I had brought back from my trip. It was fun putting it together, and it helped make Mexico come alive for my students. When we studied South America, one of my students brought in a jungle-type net. We hung it from the ceiling, and the students brought in stuffed animals from that part of the world. It covered the whole ceiling. These are the kinds of things teachers do all the time."

Kate Companik taught reading in her elementary classroom the same way for 18 years. In her nineteenth year she decided it was time for a change. At International Reading Association meetings she had been learning about incorporating reading with other subject areas and how to use literature to teach kids to read. She began with some theories and ideas and built from there. What amazed her was how all the pieces started to come together.

"I began changing my reading program by utilizing literature books to teach reading rather than the basals, focusing on themes and on certain authors of children's literature, incorporating more writing, incorporating the use of journals, and getting away from workbooks in reading, spelling, and language. This was a big change, and I didn't know how it would all fall into place.

One day a student said, 'Why is it whenever we're doing something that it always goes along with something we're doing somewhere else?' He could see the connections. He noticed that one of our spelling words was also a concept we were studying in science. And what we were studying in science was in the literature book we were reading. In *James and the Giant Peach* by Roald Dahl, James's friends are Centipede, Old-Green-Grasshopper, Miss Spider, Glow-worm, Earthworm, Silkworm, and Ladybug. We were studying insects in science. We worked in groups research-ing each insect, wrote reports, and used a grid to enlarge the insect. We also discussed habitat and food chains. As we read the book the author would include information about the insects which the children always noticed. They would refer back to their research to verify these facts. When it was explained in the book that long-horned grasshop-pers 'sing' by rubbing the bases of their wings together and that they hear with their legs, and that short-horned grasshoppers make noise by rubbing their hind legs against their wings, my kids got so excited because we had learned that in science.

"Much that passes for education . . . is not education at all but ritual. The fact is that we are being educated when we know it least."   David P. Gardner, President, University of Utah

That was really exciting for me. It helped me see that it was coming togeth-er, that my planning was paying off. When a student says something like, 'Hey, wait a minute, weren't we working on that in science and now we're doing it in our literature book?' I can see they're catching the connection.

Sometimes connections just happened that I haven't planned. I'm not sure how to describe it, but you start with an idea, and that idea kind of snowballs and moves into new ideas, and you just keep going and it all falls into place. You didn't realize it was going to, and it's fun. I like it. I am not even sure sometimes when I start something how everything's going to pull together, but it comes together perfectly. That's what's exciting for me—to pull ideas togeth-er and get them to work."

While some good teachers learn how to make the puzzle pieces fit quite nicely, others of us may have had to work a little harder to get the hang of it. This often becomes an advantage as we can more easily relate to the struggling student or the beginning teacher. Determining ways to handle some of the mundane tasks that come with our jobs will do a lot to help make our lives easier.

I (Ginny) remember my first experience in a junior high classroom. I'd been told there were footprints on the teacher's desk. Some out-of-control student, the informant told me. After being in the classroom a number of seconds, I decided it was probably the sub's footprints, struggling to find a way out of this chaos. My mind's eye could see her clearly, holding her skirt tightly around her, gracelessly pole vaulting up to the desk, holding her hands to her ears, screaming for help. The students were dancing around the desk, chanting, clapping their hands and stomping their feet in time to their horrifying noises.

A level of sound similar to that of an approaching freight train brought me quickly back to the present. What was I doing here? Two and a half months into the school year, this classroom had gone through two teachers and numerous substitutes. Did this mean nothing to me? I questioned my own sanity. But here I was, another warm body for these junior high Rambos to try to destroy.

The first year I survived. And that's about all I can say about it. There were more days than I care to remember when I cried on the commute home from school; on the way to my classes, I prayed long and hard for the strength to make it through the hours ahead. But I was determined to do more than simply survive, so I began to look for some answers.

I learned that junior high students need structure. I also found that they respond well to fairness and positive consequences for effort put forth. I decided to give them healthy doses of each. I borrowed a system from a veteran junior high teacher which seemed to be what I needed. It would provide consistent structure, would help teach organization, and would give students who try a chance to do well.

In my seventh- and eighth-grade English classes, students get a maximum of five daily attendance points, one each for having a pencil, a red correction pen or pencil, a bound folder, a leisure reading book, and a daily agenda (calendar planner). In addition, students get a maximum of five points daily for the folder assignment (textbook assignment, mini-lesson skills sheet, etc.) completed. In a particular week, there may be four folder assignments and one hand-in assignment, which is collected and graded for percentage points. If the student's folder assignment is only half finished, he gets only three points. More than half earns him four points, while less than half earns him two; and if he had barely begun, he gets one point. Students trade papers to determine these homework points. So that the students don't take these points too lightly, I take the time in the beginning to show them how these will work into their grade, explaining that a four or a three may not sound too bad in comparison to a total of five points, but when they look at percentages, they will see an 80 percent or a 60 percent. When those numbers are consistently averaged into grades, it will make an impact.

Each day of class, we take points orally immediately after students are seated. They are on an honor system. If it is discovered that a student is being untruthful, he loses all of his points for that day. I have had classes in which I have discontinued these participation points for a period of time because students have taken advantage of it, but overall it has worked well, and the students realize its benefits. The procedure may be a bit hectic for a few days until students get a feel for it, but it will soon run very smoothly, and students will be comfortable with it.

An additional method, added later in my years with junior high students, involves reading and composition. I conference with each student as he or she sets goals for the number of books to be read during the quarter and the writing skills on which he will work. Students keep literature logs (kept in a spiral notebook) in which they write brief letters to me about their reading. They are to write once a week and place the writing in a basket on my desk. I respond and place the notebooks in a box in the back of my room which is marked for each class. Students comment on the plot of the story, the characters involved, their own feelings about how the author handles certain situations or how they feel about what is happening in the story. I answer the students' comments with a short note of my own. I have been much happier with this type of "evaluation" of reading than with the traditional book report, and have noticed also that writing skills continue to improve. Each Monday I "check" the lit logs simply by calling students up to my desk to see what they are reading and having them show me their letter with my response. Since they can turn logs in at any time, I am not bombarded with all responses at one time. Occasionally, if a week is particularly hectic, I give them some "time off" or request that they write to friends or family members for responses.

I feel that this system is a fair one, and I am convinced that it helps those students who are hard workers and who try to achieve but may have some problems in particular areas. It also helps students learn to organize, which is often a problem for junior high students. I admit that this is not a foolproof method, as every quarter some students continually miss points because of forgotten materials or incomplete work. But overall, I feel confident that it is beneficial.

Learning a system such as the one I've mentioned helped me to succeed in gaining order and structure in my classroom, but it took time to fit the pieces together. Today I do not necessarily follow all of the components of this plan. My classroom and my teaching has evolved with my own growth, but it was a very strong, basic foundation that contributed to my students' achievements as well as my own. When the puzzle pieces don't seem to fit, open your eyes and ears and look within. Answers will come, and your life will be easier.

Fuel for the Fire
IDEAS TO INCORPORATE

- Read help books that discuss techniques and practical suggestions for teachers. Find a teacher who is strong in your area of weakness and ask questions and observe. Then do some self-evaluating and follow through with action.
- Look at your own personality and hobbies. Look for ways to incorporate something you enjoy as a hobby into your teaching. For example, if you are a gardener, grow plants in your room for science.
- Take advantage of those times in the classroom when you don't have the answers to your students' questions. Seize these opportunities to show students your own thinking processes to model how to became lifelong learners.
- Teacher and students can research together to build upon their knowledge in certain areas. Give your students an interest inventory to find out what their interests are. Interest inventories can be made quickly and easily. They are often a list of questions such as "What kinds of movies do you like? What are your favorite books or television shows? What is your favorite activity to do at home (other than watch TV)? What places would you like to visit? What are your hobbies? What sports do you like?" Look for common areas of interest that you can study as a class. Design a unit around it.
- Go back to school to take a class you are interested in. It may even be a noncredit course.

- Read a newspaper regularly. Look for things you can incorporate into your class.
- Use Ann Werland's idea: Choose a topic about which you want to learn more. Put it on the board on Monday for an extra-credit assignment. Give students until Friday to research and write a brief report on the topic.
- Look at workshop or conference opportunities of interest to you. Mark them on your calendar and plan to attend at least one. Find a colleague to join you and ask your administration for money to attend.
- Rework some of your classroom curriculum to include new material, ideas, or projects.
- Using the book *Aunt Flossie's Hats*, let students make hats to match those in the story. Hats can be made out of Styrofoam bowls or Styrofoam cups, which, when heated, melt to look like small hats. Students can also write their own stories and make hats to match their stories.
- Provide opportunities for your students to teach something to the class based on their knowledge, interest, and expertise. Confer with them ahead of time to help guide their subject matter. I (Beth) do this with my classes of preservice secondary education teachers. Students are to teach short 20-minute lessons from their subject areas. The only requirement is that they can't just tell us; we have to be doing something because we learn by doing. We have every major represented in the classes—English, math, music, agriculture, the sciences, history—so we learn information as well as learning from a variety of teaching styles. We have learned about geometry and origami from the math teachers, how to march in formation from the band instructors, and how to make paper from the art teachers. It's interesting, educational, and fun.
- Play "stump the teacher," in which you and the students take turns asking questions about a chapter you've read or unit you've studied. You can guide the level of questioning by asking higher level questions on your turn and encouraging students to ask more than literal or factual questions. Students will read the material carefully in order to try to "stump" you. Keep score - teacher vs. students.
- Are there lessons your students have taught you without their knowing it? Think of some situations where you have learned some truths from your charges. When you learn something from your students, be sure to tell them. This shows that learning is not one-sided in your classroom, and that learning is a lifelong process.

Just for the Preservice Teacher

- Create an interest inventory to give to your future students.
- Start a collection of items from college or vacations that you can use in your classroom the way Dianne Renkoski did with her trip to Mexico.
- On the left side of a piece of paper, make a list of the characteristics of a teacher. On the right side of the page, make a list of your personality traits. Count how many you have that are in both columns. Do you have characteristics that fit well with teaching?

Discovering the Rewards of Diversity

Cultural diversity. Multiculturalism. The buzzwords of the day. We are told as teachers that we need to teach our students about diversity. Perhaps before we can teach our students to respect those of a different color or culture, we must first teach them to respect those around them who have different tastes, temperaments, or opinions. This concept was beautifully illustrated recently in a fifth-grade classroom that I (Beth) visited. I was observing a student teacher who was introducing the concept of diversity. Renee Cook began by writing the word "diversity" on the board using a different color of chalk for each letter. She then asked students what they thought the word meant. The answers varied, but none quite captured the intent.

"There may be said to be two classes of people in the world: those who constantly divide the people of the world into two classes, and those who do not."
Benchley

Renee then held up a beautiful patchwork quilt and asked the students to describe it. They spoke up about the many different colors, the different shapes, sizes, and designs. Renee went on to say that it took all of the pieces sewn together to make up the beauty and the charm of the quilt. She told the class that that is how diversity works—that different people together make this a beautiful world.

Renee gave the students a sheet of paper and asked them to list things about themselves such as their favorite sports, television shows, or what they want to be when they grow up. Then she called on two students to read their lists. The two lists were entirely different. Renee asked the class if the fact that they had such different interests meant they shouldn't like each other. The class laughed and thought that was silly. So Renee explained that that is what diversity means—understanding one another's differences.

Renee culminated the unit by asking each student to make a "quilt block" on a sheet of paper which represented who they are. She then tied the "blocks" together with string to make a class quilt. The students in the fifth-grade class learned an important lesson from their teacher about the value of each individual.

Cheryl Afghanipour has a passion for helping her students gain a broader perspective of cultural diversity. She teaches in an inner-city middle school that is made up predominantly of minority students. Cheryl feels that many of the problems in her school are racially motivated, and that one of the differences she can make is to help her students recognize the uniqueness of each individual. Because of her own interest in this area, she has created multicultural units that fit into every subject area she teaches. She has been able to pass along some of her own enthusiasm to students who become more knowledgeable about other cultures.

"I've always believed that understanding other cultures is the only way we will have peace as a society. We must have an understanding of each other's culture and be respectful of our likenesses and differences. I have learned that often people may feel that others show prejudice toward them, but they do not understand that they may be making the same kinds of judgments toward other groups. It is important that they recognize their own prejudices before real growth can occur.

Each month I concentrate on specific ethnic contributions to society. We also study music, religion, dress, food, holidays, and other appropriate cultural knowledge. By the end of the year, students have a better grip on cultural influence.

One exercise I do with my students seems to make a lasting impression on them. I boil brown-shelled and white-shelled eggs. We make a Venn diagram while discussing the differences and similarities between the two eggs. As the class observes, I shell the eggs. I hold up the shelled eggs and ask, 'Can you tell which egg is from the brown shell and which is from the white?' In most cases, students think there will be some way they will be able to distinguish between the two, but as they observe, they discover that, no, they don't know which is which. I then slice the eggs. 'Look inside. Now, can you tell which egg is which?' Again, they must admit they can't. I tell the students, 'This is what I'm trying to say—inside we are all the same; all of us need to be loved and cared for.' This is a concept that is very important to me, and I am able to pass that enthusiasm on to my students."

Individuals Build a Team

Marcia Hansen works with her team of middle school teachers to help their students understand that we need to help all of those around us including those who might be different from ourselves.

"*O*ur team teaches six different units a year. Our kids learn and grow with each unit. It is exciting to see our kids use what they have learned beyond our classroom. An example of their team spirit was evidenced one year during intramural sports. Our kids were playing a game called 'Poison River.' It involved the whole group moving from one side of the gym to the other, crossing only on small pieces of carpet placed across the room because the floor was 'poisonous.' A member of our team had a physical disability and as a result her legs were not nearly as long as the rest of the team members'. When it was her turn to cross the river, the squares were too far apart for her. She jumped to the first square and then her team members bodily picked her up and handed her from member to member across the 'poison river.' I know my kids will be faced with a lot of 'poison rivers' after they leave my class. I sleep better at night knowing that our students have learned that sometimes you lift someone else up and sometimes you have to let someone else help you."

"No race can prosper till it learns that there is as much dignity in tilling a field as in writing a poem."
Booker T. Washington

The "teamwork" at Marcia Hansen's school broadens learning in other ways.

"Middle school is teamwork. Teachers and students form a team that is supported by parents, administrators, and staff who all work together to create a positive learning experience. The ultimate goal of our team is to create a 'family' for the students. We know the power of a family. Everyone wants to be accepted unconditionally, to have others who want you to succeed, to be missed when you are gone, and to have a history with someone. I think building this kind of relationship creates a bond of love between the students and the teacher that remains in our hearts forever.

Our school year starts with three teachers and 60 to 70 students in our team. Some of the students know one another, and others don't know anyone. Some students are gifted academically and others are remedial. Some students have it together socially and others have no social skills whatsoever. There are those with behavior disorders or physical disabilities and those we would call average. Some students come from 'Leave It to Beaver' homes while others have parole officers and sleep in cars on cold nights. The goal is to find a way to make a family out of these very diverse kids.

We teachers meet daily to plan and work for our team of kids. We have been most successful in building the 'family' by involving students in our teaching units and thematic teaching. For example, we always begin the school year with 'The Cookbook Company' unit. The team of teachers and students writes and produces a cookbook full of their favorite recipes and original poems. The students borrow anywhere from $800 to $1,000 from a local bank. They plan their own marketing strategies to sell the cookbooks. The kids are responsible for paying off the loan and spending their profit money wisely.

"We are not a melting pot, but a beautiful mosaic. Different people, different beliefs, different yearning, different hopes, different dreams."
Jimmy Carter

This unit does so much for our kids. The obvious is that they learn about writing, editing, and poetry in language arts; the chemistry of cooking in science; measurement in math; and economics in social studies. But just as important, students gain such a sense of pride and accomplishment. What begins as just an idea from their teachers ends up making them at least $1,000 profit. This empowers kids and proves to them they can do anything.

Students also learn to appreciate the strengths of their classmates and to accept one another's weaknesses. They begin to see the 'big picture' and will overcome problems or personal needs for the good of the 'company.' For example, one of our students, who typically dressed in the latest grunge attire, donned a conservative shirt and dress pants on the day the loan officer came to interview the students.

The less popular but more capable students will be hired by the class as company managers. Students know that managers will be getting bids and talking to the bank. They want the best person for the job, not the most popular student.

I sit in on the manager's meeting in which the assembly lines are hired. Each manager is responsible for a portion of the line. Each selects his or her workers, trains them, and keeps them on task until the book is assembled. I hear comments the managers make like, 'I can't have _____ on my line. We are too good of friends, we might goof off,' or 'I'll take him, he gets along well with me and the others on my line. If he gets mad at you, he'll slow down your line.'"

The day of production I see the assembly line working as smoothly as any factory. Kids will be working as hard and as fast as they can for three solid hours. We often have to make them take a break. I see students who wouldn't do an assignment in class if their lives depended on it inspecting cookbooks with the diligence of Bob Cratchit.

The students always have a press conference to kick off the book sales. We used to hand-select students who might be asked to interview on camera, wanting those who know what is going on. We have come to realize that all of our students can explain what they have learned; they all know. Imagine if I were teaching economics from a textbook and a news team showed up to ask my students what they had learned!

I am fired up about teaching this year and the next and the one after that. It is amazing to watch this mass of unlike kids mesh together into a family. At the end of the year I am so proud of each student. I know how far some of my kids had to grow and stretch, and I also know how far others had to bend down to lend a hand. And I am filled with pride that I am part of that family, and that I had a hand in helping create it."

Moving Beyond Labels

Chris Craig, teacher and department head in a university Department of Reading and Special Education, views disabilities as "simply another form of human diversity."

"My perspective on diversity is based on experiences as an individual who is totally blind and as one with over 16 years of teaching children and youth with disabilities. In my view, our society has yet to evolve to the point where disability is viewed merely as another form of human diversity in the same way as we think about race, religion, national origin, or gender. It is human nature to focus on that which is exceptional about an individual while excluding all other relevant facts. I have been described as a musician, parent, college professor, and a Star Trek enthusiast who happens to be blind. Although most people tend to focus initially on the fact that I use alternative techniques for travel or reading such as a white cane or my Braille material, blindness is simply one of my characteristics and clearly not the essence of who I am.

Judicial rulings and laws such as the Americans with Disabilities Act (ADA) and the Individuals with Disabilities Education Act (IDEA) do little to 'keep the light in the eyes' of teachers as it relates to diversity. Language, however, is the essence of culture and does have the power to change ideas and perspectives. Thus, the first step in learning to regard disability as part of the diversity mosaic of the classroom is to look at the person first before the disability that may or may not impact learning. Labels are for cans, not people, but they are a necessary part of our system for identifying children who need specialized instruction and in securing funding for programming.

There are certain things I can't control, but there are things that I can. I focus on those things. You can't worry about what you can't control. I can't control being blind, so I accept it and don't worry. There's a difference between acceptance and succumbing. You don't let your disabilities set your limitations. This is what I try to teach students who also have disabilities. You develop coping systems over time to compensate for what you can't do. Even though I haven't seen a face in 25 years, I have learned the importance of eye contact and facial expressions. It is a learned behavior. We teach students skills such as this to help them succeed. Some people really identify with their disability. It becomes who they are. I don't want to view my disability as who I am and I teach students to do the same.

When dealing with any kind of diversity, I rely strongly on principles taught by Stephen Covey in *Seven Habits for Highly Effective People,* such as seeking first to understand rather than seeking to be understood. When working with children, or anyone for that matter, I can't make any judgment clearly until I understand where they are coming from. I look at the issues before I express my own views. I work hard at this."

Ann Alofs teaches second and third grade in a school with a diverse population of students.

"The diversity of my classroom . . . I never really think about it very much. The biggest part of my class is from a low socioeconomic background, but I'd have to see my kids if I were to count how many students from what culture I have in my room. A few weeks ago, a parent said to me, 'My child said he is the only white boy in your room; is that true?' I honestly didn't know for sure. I had to go back and look. And he wasn't.

Cultural diversity is not the only diversity I see in my classroom. I have many families with religious diversities as well. 'John' is a nine-year-old African American boy whose mother sees the world in a very strict Christian/fundamentalist view. John is not allowed to participate in any Halloween activities, and his mom and I have talked extensively about my curriculum and the possible hidden 'evils' here. I've tactfully explained to John's mother that choral reading is different from satanic chanting and has value in the public schools. On the other hand, 'Gaia' is an eight-year-old, blond-haired girl from a very eclectic Pagan family. For sharing time one day she brought in pictures of various goddesses and told the other children about goddesses in her religion. When it came time for a new seating arrangement, I felt it was time for everyone to broaden their horizons, so, John, the fundamentalist Christian, and Gaia, the Pagan, sat next to each other—sharing crayons, offering advice on how to spell 'friend,' and getting along very, very well."

Language Is Only the Beginning

Kathy Brady is an English as a Second Language (ESL) teacher at a large university, so to her, diversity is the name of the game. Kathy's students come from all over the world. A typical class might consist of thirteen students who come from nine different countries and speak eight different languages. They are there primarily because they want to study at a United States university, and they need to improve their language in order to pass a standardized test of English proficiency (TOEFL) before they will be admitted to a university here. Kathy says:

"Language diversity is the oil that keeps our program running smoothly. If no two students in a class speak the same language, there is a real and critical need to communicate in English. On the other hand, if most of the students share a language, English seems like a game, and we lose the sense of urgency. (Students will do the required work in English, but then turn to their classmates and ask in their native language what their lunch plans are.) Language diversity, then, solves some of the problems that might exist in a monolingual language classroom. Other areas (cultural diversity and social diversity) can be more challenging.

When people from different cultures come together, there are inevitable misunderstandings. Our culture shapes so much of our daily interaction that we can't really escape it. We know when to shake hands with people to greet them, when to give a big hug, or when to just smile and nod. We don't have to think about it—in fact, it's often not possible to think about it because these guidelines are so ingrained and are so much a part of who we are that we don't even recognize that they're there. The biggest reason that misunderstandings arise, then (in my opinion), is that we act—subconsciously and unknowingly—out of these rules of our culture and we aren't aware that we are doing so—or, more importantly, that those rules are different in other cultures. When another person doesn't follow the same rules, it grates on us, but we aren't usually able to explain why. In our culture, we look our conversation partner in the eyes when we talk. In many other cultures, a student, particularly, never looks his or her teacher in the eyes. It would be extremely disrespectful to do so. Both people are uncomfortable during conversations, but neither knows why.

Teaching in a situation like this is a little like juggling water balloons. Park challenges everything I say the first days of class. In his culture, women are seldom or never in a position of authority over men. I have to be firm and in control but not alienate him. Juan and Abdullah begin to shout out an answer to my questions before I've even finished them, while Lee and Chang sit silently, looking annoyed. The typical 'wait time' in their cultures differs. To Juan and Abdullah, it indicates a lack of interest if they don't respond immediately. To Lee and Chang, immediate response shows a lack of thoughtfulness about the answer, and thus a lack of respect for the teacher. In classes where this an issue, I talk openly about it. Understanding the cultural differences doesn't change students' behavior, necessarily, but it makes it easier for them to tolerate one another—and me! In general, I think it's important to be as open as possible about potentially difficult issues. We talk about them, examine them, help one another understand them. It's also important for me to be able to use humor—we all have to laugh at ourselves—but humor has its own dangers in a multicultural setting and has to be used very carefully.

"After all, there is but one race—humanity." George Moore

At the end of the year, we host a picnic or party for our students. Typically, in the spring, we hire a square-dance caller who teaches them American folk dances. Latin American, African, Middle Eastern, Asian, and European students struggle with their hardest 'listening comprehension' exercise of the semester and dutifully 'swing their partner and do-si-do.' Afterward, we learn to do the samba or listen to mournful songs of the Ud.

I think it's essential for my students to know and 'feel' deep down that I respect them. I am not going to try to change them, but I want to help them survive in this classroom and in this culture. I don't tolerate any negative comments directed toward other students. They have to show respect for one another within my classroom. For us to work together, the classroom has to be a 'safe place' where no one fears being humiliated if he or she makes a mistake. There is also no exclusivity allowed. No two people are allowed to speak a language that no one else understands. For the most part, I'm amazed at how well these classes mesh. Watching this many diverse people work so well together and actually develop friendships that they carry with them out of the program gives me hope for the future of the world. I sometimes tell my students that I feel we're a mini-United Nations that could serve as a model for the real one."

Janet R. Zupon has taught first grade for 20 years. She herself experienced the situation of being a minority in a different culture when she was a foreign-exchange student in Paraguay. Janet has received the Excellence in Teaching Award and was her district's finalist for the Teacher of the Year Award. She shares her own methods of successfully working with ESL students.

"Working with ESL students is a rewarding challenge. They have special needs that vary greatly depending on how long they have been in the country and how much English is spoken at home. Students who have just arrived in the country or who have not been in the school environment need time to explore and learn the social behaviors expected at school. Helping the other students accept this learning process is also part of my job. I have allowed my ESL students to explore the room when we are having a lesson that is very language dependent. I've never encouraged this exploration, but since we have our own bathroom, it seems to occur naturally. My ESL students often stop at the math manipulatives, computer, or reading centers on their way back from the bathroom. After a short explanation about how this helps the ESL students understand our classroom, the other students are very accepting. Sometimes I send another child to 'explain the centers'—encouraging talking and gesturing to the ESL student.

I always assign an interested student to be a 'buddy.' The buddy has an important job—always to know where the ESL student is and to be sure he or she is safe. I choose responsible, verbal, and empathetic buddies. They make sure their ESL students don't get lost at lunch, in hallways, etc. It makes lines a little noisy, but the payoff is great. The buddy also gains a sense of pride in his or her own responsibility as well as the buddy's progress.

Lunch is often a challenge with ESL students. Expecting an accurate lunch count is not realistic. I speak with the cafeteria manager and explain that the ESL students will need to see the food and then choose. ESL students often are unsure about new foods. Someone needs to watch to be sure that they actually eat. I've seen ESL students spit out food and gag on foods that are new to them. Playground rules often may be taught by modeling and a firm 'no' when safety rules are violated. Fellow students are very helpful in showing appropriate behavior.

School supplies and library books are also sources of confusion. ESL students may pack their school supplies to take them home. If they don't have these items at home, it may be helpful to see if PTA will donate items from the school store. It's very difficult to explain about taking things home and bringing them back. It's best if library books and school supplies remain at school until someone can communicate the need for the timely return of these items.

ESL students who speak English fairly well can often be successful in the regular classroom. Directions will sometimes need to be repeated, simplified, or modeled clearly to ensure success. Helping the ESL student get started is a little extra that really pays off. The ESL students may not ask for help. They may copy or not get started if they are unsure. Remember when you assign homework that there may not be anyone at home who can work with the ESL student. Using an older student at school or the buddy system may be a better alternative.

Having ESL students in your class offers a wealth of opportunities to learn about other cultures and languages. Gather helpful information from your ESL teacher. You need to know things such as Chinese students don't want you to touch them on the head. Some students may fast as part of a religious holiday, and they shouldn't be pressured to eat. Teachers and students can share in respecting cultural differences. We also enjoy academic opportunities. Geography comes to life as we locate continents and countries where your ESL students once lived. We also enjoy learning to count in different languages. Students learn about different holidays and ways of celebrating them. A class is really enriched by the addition of ESL students.

Being a successful teacher with ESL students depends more on attitude than skill. Accepting and rejoicing in growth is imperative. Accepting mistakes and deviations from routine with a sense of humor is a great asset. All children are unique. Plan your program to meet their needs and everyone will have a successful year."

Fuel for the Fire
IDEAS TO INCORPORATE

- Try the "egg experiment" with your class as Cheryl Afghanipour did. Bring in brown and white boiled eggs and let your students make Venn diagrams. Then put your students into pairs and have them make a Venn diagram about their own likenesses and differences.
- Talk with other teachers about ways you can work together as a team. Plan activities for your students to do together. Or work with art, music, PE, or other teachers about ways to integrate their subjects into your own.

- Bring multicultural literature into your classroom and make it a part of as many lessons as possible. This will help your students get a broader picture of our world and help you celebrate diversity.
- Plan a unit in which your students study their own heritage and culture. Have students make short presentations to the class about their diverse backgrounds. Be sure you take a turn, too, to let your students know more about you.
- When studying different cultures, have students learn a few phrases from the language of that culture. If possible, bring in guests to share stories and information.
- Take advantage of student book clubs to purchase multicultural books and literature sets for your class library.
- Attend multicultural and diversity workshops in your area to learn new ways to make the study of other cultures a part of your everyday curriculum.

Just for the Preservice Teacher

- Begin now to start building your own multicultural library. Look for books that you can integrate into your future curriculum.
- Most universities offer workshops and seminars on multicultural issues. Look for them and attend as many as possible.

Dealing with Issues
of Discipline

Training your students to develop self-control and
responsibility does not come easily, but is well worth
the time spent.

Teachers coming into a school system from their college classrooms over-
whelmingly agree they are not prepared for many of the routine tasks they
face in and out of the classroom. One of the most difficult areas is dealing
with discipline. Exactly what is discipline? People often mistakenly believe
that discipline and punishment are synonymous. That is not the case.
Discipline trains. Webster's dictionary defines discipline as "training that
develops self-control, character, or orderliness and efficiency."
Consequences are an important part of discipline. Students must learn that
there are natural consequences for breaking rules. But punishment is only a
piece of the puzzle.

New teachers often struggle with classroom management. Many leave
the profession with feelings of frustration and even bitterness when their
attempts at effectively handling their students have failed. In his book *Dare
to Discipline*, James Dobson states: "It has been estimated that 80 percent of
the teachers who quit their jobs after their first year do so because of an
inability to maintain discipline in their classroom." This figure wouldn't
surprise a teacher. Those of us who remain in the classroom know that if we
don't maintain discipline, it doesn't matter what creative teaching techniques or what innovative methods we employ; we cannot teach if we don't
have our students' attention.

Veteran teachers admit that we are living in a new era in education.
Today, we are forced to deal with issues that our peers even a generation
ago did not face. Margaret LeCompte, co-author of *Giving up on School:
Teacher Burnout and Student Dropout*, reports that "teachers are being
trained for the 1930s school, but they are experiencing 1990s kids and
1990s society."

I (Beth) was once discussing with my mother-in-law some discipline
problems I was having with a student. She made a statement that has stuck
with me. She said that when she was a young girl, her mother's first question when she came in the door after her first day of school was, "Does
the teacher like you?" Now, the question asked
by parents is, "Do you like your teacher?" That
rang true. That is what I ask my own kids. When
I was young, if I got in trouble at school, I was in
a lot more trouble when I got home. Now, it
seems that when a child gets in trouble at school, parents are quick to
blame the teacher (at least that's what we heard from many teachers). The
cause of this shift may be attributed to many factors, but no matter the
cause, the fact remains that we as teachers must deal with change. Some

"The art of being wise is the
art of knowing what to
overlook." William James

teachers seem to have an innate ability to deal with discipline issues, while others do not. However, these methods can be learned through experience and the advice and examples of other teachers who have dealt with similar problems.

A myriad of books exist on the subject of discipline in the classroom, and philosophies have swung back and forth on the pendulum since the beginning of public education. The purpose of this section is not to persuade you to agree with one expert's belief over another's. Our purpose is to show, through the experiences of successful teachers, ideas to help in difficult situations so that you aren't held captive by a classroom that is out of control.

Students Benefit from Consistency

Our word must mean something to our students. It is essential that we think before we speak, and that we only make promises we can keep. Consistency means more than just following through with what we say. It also means acting in a way that corresponds with our expectations. If we don't want our students to belittle one another, then it is imperative that we avoid put-downs ourselves. Our students need to see us practicing what we preach lest our words become meaningless. Ralph Waldo Emerson said, "Who you are shouts so loudly I cannot hear what you say."

We lose our validity when our students hear us saying one thing and doing another.

Our students watch us very closely. A student in one of my (Ginny's) eighth-grade English classes brought this point home in a note he wrote in his literature journal. He had been reading some of the works of Confucius, and I asked him to respond to what he was reading. When I received his journal, one of the comments he had penned was, "Confucius often contradicted his philosophy by his own actions. In short, Confucius did not follow himself! So how can anything that he uttered be true?" He followed this statement with some contradictory examples of Confucius's quotes and his lifestyle. Inconsistencies don't slip by our students.

Mary Wright says that her students taught her the importance of consistency and ultimatums.

"A lesson I learned early in my teaching career was to be very careful before you give a strict ultimatum, saying, 'If you don't do this, you'll have to do that.' In the most trying situations I allow some time to distance myself from the problem and arrive at a logical and helpful solution. My first year as a teacher with many young charges, I learned that the louder I got, the louder they became. I realized one day that I did not have control, and drastic steps needed to be taken if any learning was going to happen. One day, as a class came in acting as though they were still on the playground, I attempted to take roll and get them ready to work. They were so loud that my voice couldn't be heard above the din.

"Children are unpredictable. You never know what inconsistency they're going to catch you in next."
Franklin P. Jones

I quietly pulled out my chair, sat down, and started writing the name of anyone I saw talking. In a very calm, soft voice, I told them the consequences for their inability to be quiet. As I continued to talk consequences and write names, I began to hear shh's, and quietness came in waves over the room; they were able to hear what I was saying. 'Each person whose name is on this paper (by then, all names were there) will be required to stay after school 15 minutes for every minute it took this class to get quiet.' They stayed after school that day. Many students missed the bus and had to walk several miles home.

In today's world of rights and lawsuits, teachers must be careful what ultimatums they give, because once you say you will do something, you must follow through. In this case, my classes did learn they needed to be quiet in math class, and both they and I learned that getting louder won't create order; it only increases disorder."

Students Benefit from Boundaries and Need to Know Someone Is in Control

A story was told about a fence that had been built around a schoolyard. Believing that the children might feel confined, it was decided to remove the boundary. After the removal, school authorities noticed that the children were huddling together in the middle of the playground; they evidently did not feel the freedom to wander across the schoolyard as they had before. The contractors soon rebuilt the fence. Before long, children were again running and playing throughout the playground. Children and young people, no matter the age, need the guidance and safety of boundaries. As teachers, we must realize this and provide appropriate limits.

We teach students how to set their own boundaries when we set boundaries in our classrooms.

Most of us have stories of students or situations that have challenged us. The best ones, though, are of those that have come back to us as rewards. They keep us motivated. Janice Hogan is the principal of a junior high and high school. She was recently informed that her school system is going to name their newly built library after her. Quite an honor. It took her awhile to get to that point, and she will never forget her first year as a classroom teacher.

"You want to talk about a challenge? My first teaching job came along in the middle of a school year, February to be exact. I accepted a position in a small town with a population of less than 1,000. I was the fourth social studies teacher in the junior high/high school during this particular year. I was told that the first teacher that year was fired in December because she had no control in her classes. The second teacher hired told the superintendent that 'life was too short to endure the behavior of these students.' Within two weeks, she had walked out and never returned.

They hired me as a substitute until a certified social studies teacher could be found. I had the required certification but absolutely no experience. I soon found out why the other teachers had hit the road. Some of the students told me to my face, 'Oh, good! Here's another teacher we can run off.' Because of the situation and teacher turnover during the school year, even students who wouldn't normally be discipline problems joined the crowd.

It was me and them; it was scary. To complicate matters, the teaching materials were slim to none. Not all students had textbooks and many of those available were very outdated.

To illustrate how bad the situation was, let me tell you about a day during my second week of teaching. This particular event took place in a citizenship class with 35 students. I had five students who had been absent and missed a test. I had arranged for the students to make up the test in the study hall that met right across the hall. I escorted the students to the room and gave the study hall teacher their tests. When I walked back into my classroom (I had been gone less than 30 seconds), the classroom was absolutely quiet. My desk and chair had been moved against the blackboard. Books from a bookshelf in the back of the room had been thrown to the front of the room. The pencil sharpener, which was screwed into the door facing, had been jerked out of the wall (screws and all) and had been thrown to the floor.

These students wanted me to show my fear and how upset I was when I entered the classroom and found such a mess. I decided quickly that I was not going to give them the reactions they expected. I did not show my fear, my anger, my frustration, my desire to kill everyone of them. Instead, I remained calm. I had a couple of the boys help me clean up.

All students had their eyes on me, waiting to see me explode, cry, or both. I did neither. I talked calmly (to this day I'm not sure how I did this), determined not to give them the reaction they were hoping for. After the mess was picked up, I talked calmly to the class. I told them that I was not leaving. I was staying. I was in charge of the classroom and I would give them only the freedom that they could handle. Obviously, they could not handle a reading assignment while I was out of the room for 30 seconds.

Things did not completely turn around at that point. I sought the advice of experienced teachers and my administration. From these sources I developed a plan that helped the students and me to be successful with disciplinary issues. I announced to my students that if anyone came to class continually without materials (pencil, paper, and textbook), or if a student was uncooperative or insubordinate, that student would be removed from the classroom and could not return until a conference with the parent, student, and myself. This worked wonders.

The first student I ejected was the child of a school board member. When that parent came in for the conference, this student's behavior changed dramatically. As I had more parent conferences, my classroom became a place of learning.

Most parents were very supportive. However, not all were. When you have a parent's support, the student's behavior changes quickly. When you don't, changes can still be made effectively by sticking to your guns, letting students know what your expectations are, what you will and will not allow. When you insist that you have to have a classroom environment where all students can learn and no student has the right to disrupt the education of all students, parents can't argue with this philosophy.

Although my teaching career started out in such a challenging environment, I found success and rewards. I have remained in this same school system for 20 years. My success as a teacher and now as an administrator has resulted from being firm, fair, friendly, and consistent."

Children and young adults alike desire order in the classroom; they want the security of knowing their dignity will be protected. Someone will fill this role of controller, and if it isn't the teacher, it will be some student or students. Those teachers who maintain order, especially without being tyrannical, are usually the ones students most respect. At the beginning of the year, it is important to establish your role; make it clear to the students exactly who is in charge. In the long run, they will appreciate it, and your life will be much easier.

"The secret of success is consistency of purpose."
Benjamin Disraeli

Cindie Hendrix is a high school teacher who has the reputation of running a tight ship. She believes gaining control of the classroom is a necessity but that control must be mixed with a little love.

"I believe that there is a fine line between discipline and love. I tell my students that I love them, boys and girls alike. I use pet names like 'Sweetheart' and 'Honey.' I talk to them like I talk to my own kids. I don't believe that yelling is an answer. I can do so much with a raised eyebrow or a touch on the shoulder. The first day of school I don't pass out a sheet of paper that says these are my rules and this is what will happen if they break them. I say very quietly that I expect them to know how to behave. I don't expect them to cross any of those lines.

When students argue with me, I give them a look. They can see a change in me. For example, if someone is disrupting a lesson by talking, I might say, 'You must have a subject and a verb (Tom, stop talking) or your sentence won't be complete.' I say what I'm going to say to them, and then in the same breath go on with my lesson. It stuns them. If a student is writing a note I just go pick it up while continuing with my lesson. It gets their attention so much more. I let my students know I am disappointed. I think kids most often want to please. I try to be observant and when I realize something is going on, I acknowledge it. If you try to humiliate kids, they'll start to argue with you and you'll have problems.

Learning about the kids' backgrounds has helped me understand more about the child, and when I make it a point to show more love to that child, it helps every time. You can pull my heartstrings really easily. I am very emotional about my kids, but I'm not going to put up with any nonsense from them. They know that. I try to show them that I care. I think that makes a difference.

I tell new teachers not to worry at the very beginning about the tough academics they will need to teach. They should teach lessons they know and not try to learn new material at first. I tell them to spend their time concentrating on their classroom discipline and on gaining control and respect. They need to come in with an authoritative attitude. It's much easier to loosen up than it is to get tougher after the class is out of control."

Students Need to Know We Care and that We are Fair

Most students will accept the punishment they deserve when they know they deserve it. If we care for our students and aren't afraid to let them know it, then our fairness and firmness will make an impression that will get results. They will respond to our concern for them, and they will respect us more readily if they know that we expect it—and need it.

It is very important to kids that they be treated fairly.

Susan Shivley is a vocal music teacher in an inner-city middle school. She has learned that how she treats students has a definite effect on how they treat her.

"I have learned from working in the inner city that with these children you have to gain their confidence before they will learn from you. Their culture mandates that they are not going to respect your authority until you respect them. It's just the way it is. So I treat them all with respect, and I let them know I care about them as individuals by spending time with them, providing support they don't always get at home, and taking an interest in their lives. And they in turn respect me.

Above all else, I try to be consistent. No means no. But I also try not to tell them no. For example, when a student asks to go the rest room, instead of saying no, I say, 'Yes, as soon as the bell rings.'

I try to have fun with them and I smile and laugh a lot. Helping them to enjoy the time in my room has a big effect on discipline too."

When students recognize a teacher's concern for them, they often respond with self-discipline. Whether they consistently show it, most of our students have compassion. Mary Wright tells of a time in the 1960s when it was all she could do just to get to school and get through the day. She had been critically injured the summer before the school year in a car accident in Florida while visiting her parents. Her husband had died the spring before, leaving her with three young children to raise, and she felt that it was necessary to return to her job. She says,

"Teaching that impacts is not head to head, but heart to heart." Howard G. Hendricks

"School started with the first pre-session the day after we flew home, and the afternoon of the day I had my last cast removed. The principal had arranged for me to have a wheelchair ready that afternoon and for as long as needed. A representative from the district administration came to the meeting and said I would not be allowed to teach from a wheelchair, so I had to manage with crutches. I spent much of my time sitting, using an overhead projector. I was teaching seventh-grade reading and English. It was an amazing year, and one that has not been repeated in my 23 years of teaching. There were absolutely no discipline problems. It was a year of care and compassion.

The students' parents said they brought daily progress reports home noting each improvement, no matter how small. Many of the students asked to sit close to the front, and anytime I dropped a pencil or needed a book, there were more people ready to help than pencils in the room. It was a lesson to me in caring; they knew I cared about them. It was also a lesson in communication. Parents knew daily what was happening in the classroom, and I'm sure they helped their children see how important it was for them 'to be good.' When caring and communication fit together, I think you have found the master key for most discipline problems. Being told that they have limits gives them the boundaries they need. It's another way to say we care."

"Children have more need of models than critics."
Joseph Foubert

We Can Help Students Prevent Problems

Experience teaches us the signs of approaching trouble. We learn to recognize certain situations that will cause a disruption among our students such as a weather change or an assembly. Other warning signs may come from students who have come from a troubled situation at home, a breakup with a boyfriend or girlfriend, or simply middle school hormone horrors. The best way to avoid a problem is to recognize the potential for it and be prepared. Gwen Jeffries says,

It is easier to keep a problem from developing than it is to solve it once if has occurred.

"On the occasions when I foresee a problem and decide how to handle it, the problem never develops. Stay calm. Don't overreact. Infractions of rules are not personal attacks. The situation is rarely as serious as you make it."

Fourth-grade teacher Lori Elliott has learned an effective antidote for chaotic days.

"I stand outside my door each morning as the children come running down the hall. I can tell before I even see the whites of their eyes what kind of mood they are in. If I see backpacks swinging and arms flying, I stop the kids in the hall and deal with them before they enter the room. One day one of my girls came down the hall crying like the world had come to an end. I put a concerned arm around her and asked her what was wrong. Crying so hard she could barely talk, she said, 'My mom (sob, sob) wouldn't (sob, sob) let me (sob, sob) wear shorts today.' I said, 'Well, Cathy, it is ten degrees below zero today; don't let it ruin your day.' I have learned that if I didn't deal with Cathy right then and there then she would

"Few things help an individual more than to place responsibility upon him, and to let him know that you trust him."
Booker T. Washington

have cried and been a mess all day. This way, I addressed the issue and she could go on.

Sometimes the problems are not so frivolous. Another time a girl was upset because she was afraid she would be in trouble because her mother had not signed a note she was supposed to sign. When I asked her why her mom had not signed her note, she replied that their house had burned the night before. It was a wonder she was even at school. I would not have been in school if my house had burned.

Greeting my students at the door helps all of us set the tone for the kind of day we want to have."

Fuel for the Fire
IDEAS TO INCORPORATE

- Make a list of rules and consequences for students to follow in your classroom. Many teachers often ask students to create these during the first week of school. Students are sometimes tougher than you might be. Later, if students break the rules, remind them that they are *their* rules. Once you have a plan, stick to it. Get advice from teachers you would like to emulate. Consider your own personality and style, and devise a plan you can live with and are willing to follow.

- When a student begins to get off task or to become loud or too talkative, go stand by him or her. Your presence will quiet him and will prevent other problems from occurring.

- Look for ways to make the disruptive child the center of attention in a productive way, such as trusting her to do a special job, specifically drawing him into a discussion, asking his opinion about a topic, or catching her doing something right and commenting on it.

- Give an ultimatum only when you know you can follow through. Do what you say you will do.

- Remember that the louder you get, the louder your students will get. Demand their attention by not speaking until everyone is quiet and looking at you.

- Show respect for your students and demonstrate by your actions that you expect them to respect you (don't talk over them or down to them, don't accept rude or disrespectful responses, etc.).

- Avoid power struggles with your students. When they balk about doing something or break a rule, let them know that the choice is theirs. They may choose to do what they want, but there will be natural consequences. Make sure you find a consequence to fit the infraction and follow through. If you withdraw from the power struggle, the responsibility falls on the student, and you don't get into a nagging mode or an argument with him or her.

- If you deal with problem students publicly, they are forced to respond to you publicly. They will be more concerned about saving face in front of peers than about responding correctly to you. Whenever possible, deal with students in private either out in the hall or after class.

□ Find specific ways to let your students know you care. They will respond to this more than anything else.

Just for the Preservice Teacher

□ As you are in various schools visiting and working with children, ask teachers if you can look at their discipline rules and consequences. Ask them for advice. Keep a list of your favorite ideas to put into place when you are teaching.

□ Ask experienced teachers for ways they give students individual attention to let them know they care about them. Keep a journal in which you write down what you learn.

Avoiding the Perils of School Politics

Too much attention to school politics may hinder your effectiveness in the classroom.

While classroom management and discipline are among the most difficult issues teachers face inside the classroom, preoccupation with school politics vies as one of the most difficult aspects of teaching outside the classroom. Discouragement, disillusionment, and burnout may not be caused by students but by the clutter of the politics of the system: problems with administration, angry parents, or even participation in the gossip circles so prevalent in any work situation. Frustration may also stem from the seemingly endless changing of curricular demands, testing procedures, and teaching expectations.

For me (Beth), dealing with these issues has always been and remains one of my greatest challenges. They zap my energy and enthusiasm. After one particularly trying day I decided to make a mental note of the difference between the days when I come home from school walking on a cloud and days I feel so low I can barely walk through the door. I wanted to find out what went on at school on the good days so I could create them on a regular basis. This self-examination proved to be most interesting and confirmed some beliefs I had had all along but that I sometimes chose to ignore.

With surprising regularity, the good days were those when I had been too busy to complain to others or to hear about the latest gossip or teaching inequities. They were the days when I had been actively involved in working with my students. In looking at the days when I came home blue, I was also surprised to learn that rarely were my students the cause of my discomfort. I can manage with what goes on in my room; it's what goes on outside of my room that I struggle with.

Teachers must determine for themselves the best way to handle these complex issues of school politics. We have found that being aware of the potential for problems will help us in knowing how to deal with them when they arise. Several things are important to watch for that will help overcome the perils of school politics.

Watching What We Talk About, Think About, and Listen To

I (Beth) have looked hard to discover what makes the light begin to dim in the eyes of teachers. I do not have the answer, but I think I might be on to something. When you go into a school, listen to the "teacher talk." What they talk about is either what is stealing their passion or what is igniting their passion. For example, if teachers are always complaining about parents, students, or the principal, then that is their focus, and that is what is taking the joy out of their teaching. But if teachers are talking about those same parents, students, or the principal in a positive way, then that is what is spurring them on.

The best thing I can do for my peace of mind is to focus on my students and stay away from negative talk or negative thinking. This may mean I need to stay out of the gossip circle. Sometimes I miss that, but it's a decision I have to make. Sometimes it's a battle because my instincts are to be like Theodore Roosevelt's daughter Alice who once said, "If you don't have anything good to say about anybody, come sit by me."

"Words have no wings, but they can fly a thousand miles."
Chinese proverb

Not only must I be careful about what I listen to, I also have to watch what I talk about. I am the kind of person who can get "caught up" in talking about people and issues that frustrate me. I have to stop and remind myself to look for the good in every situation. Even if it is a situation that seems hopeless and everyone else is complaining about it, I think about teacher Nelson Parke's question, "Who says it has to be that way?" Just because other people are unhappy does not mean I have to be.

For many of us, staying out of the gossip circle is difficult. We want to know what is going on in the school. We feel "out of the loop" when we are not up to date with the latest news about who is doing what. Being in the circle also helps alleviate some of the boredom and routine of the school day and can even get our adrenaline flowing. To keep from getting pulled under by the negative influences of the gossip circle, we need to find better, more productive ways of getting our needs met.

What would the teachers in your school think if your teacher's lounge were turned into a room of encouragement? Florence Littauer, in *Silver Boxes, The Gift of Encouragement*, says that we should think of our words as "little silver boxes with bows on top—verbal presents that would encourage others."

A teacher in my (Ginny's) school has taken it upon herself to put up notes of congratulations or appreciation to other teachers. When someone walks in, he may find a note on the bulletin board congratulating him on an academic bowl or ball game victory. Or a newspaper article might be posted that focused on something or someone at the school. I recently had a piece published in our state teachers' magazine profiling another teacher in our school. In the workroom the next day I encountered a copy of the piece plastered on the refrigerator with our names highlighted and a note saying "We're proud of you." We adults enjoy pats on the back just as much as our students do, and if our "home away from home" can be a place where we hear and speak positive words, our own attitudes will be better.

"Character isn't inherited. One builds it daily by the way one thinks and acts, thought by thought, and action by action."
Helen Gahagan Douglas

Judy Just has learned in her many years of teaching that focusing on her students helps her avoid the frustrations of school politics.

"I always try to remember that my number-one priority is the kids. It's not the committee work, the school politics, the gossip in the plan room, and not worrying about which teacher might have a better schedule than I do. My focus must always be the kids. The kids are why I am there."

Esther King, first-grade teacher for 31 years, makes a special effort to be positive in her attitude and words.

"Everything you see or hear becomes a part of you. You absorb it. I think it's important not to discuss your children's problems publicly. Their problems are private to them. Children are very sensitive. I also don't want to influence the teachers who will have the students next year. It is important that they discover for themselves what these children are like.

You always have to work on being uplifting. When I'm positive with my kids, what a difference it makes, and it is like that with everybody."

Dealing Effectively with Administration

Because of varying dispositions and characteristics of teachers, principals, and superintendents, it may be a difficult task for teachers and administrators to see eye to eye. We often seem to be cut of a different piece of cloth. Yet it is to our advantage as teachers to be cooperative with our administration and to do the best we can to work together. For our own benefit, and for the good of our students, we should strive for a positive attitude and for healthy communication.

We're on the same side; let's work together.

One idea that has been productive in my (Ginny's) school is that of having a teacher who acts as a liaison between the faculty and the building principal. Vera Ker has recently acted in this capacity. She says,

"Many members of the faculty find it hard to communicate with their principals. They can't seem to share their feelings. I was the president of our local Community Teachers' Association when we had a first-year teacher who was having problems. She was not comfortable approaching the principal, and it was suggested that we have a faculty member act as a liaison between our teachers and the administrator. Another teacher and I took on this role. Several situations were brought to our attention that we were able to discuss with the building principal, and we feel that we made progress. As a result of hearing teachers' problems and concerns, we decided to begin a teacher support group to help provide some encouragement for new teachers who feel overwhelmed but are not comfortable asking for help."

Chris Blackburn, building principal in the school discussed above, agrees that having a faculty member who acts as a liaison between teachers and the administrator is helpful.

"When teachers feel uncomfortable going to the principal with a problem, it is good to have someone who can express their concern. There are times that we [administrators] aren't aware of situations, and it is beneficial to have someone who can be a voice for those who, for some reason or another, do not feel at ease talking with their administrator."

Sometimes situations with administrators are frustrating to us and seem hopeless, but we can look for ways to make the situation better. It is helpful to remember that you can't change anyone but yourself.

Our first response when we have a problem is often to blame the other person. It may be possible that the other person is at fault, but placing blame doesn't solve anything. The problem still exists. We must face the issue: There is a problem that needs to be resolved. We can't change the other person, so the change will have to come from us. Sometimes if we make a change, whether in attitude or action, the situation will improve. Think of the saying, "If nothing changes, nothing changes."

Veteran teacher June Brown has learned over the years that there are specific steps she can take to improve her relationship with administrators, enabling her to work well with them.

"One year, I had a new principal who was very quiet and difficult to get to know. Conversations with him often seemed forced and contrived. So I decided to invite him to my kindergarten class to read the book *Stone Soup* with us and to eat 'Stone Soup' (cooked in a crockpot from vegetables children brought to school). I wanted my students to share some of their new knowledge about plants from our plant unit, and they were going to perform a transformed version of the Farmer in the Dell—where a vegetable farmer takes a carrot, onion, etc.

Before his visit, I asked the children what they thought the principal's job was, and I wrote their ideas on a chart. Some of their responses were very humorous. When he came to taste our soup, he was delighted to see the children's descriptive list of his job responsibilities. It allowed him the opportunity to address some of their misconceptions as well as to see how much we were learning. He was so pleased with the list, he shared it with the main office, and somehow it ended up in the school newspaper to provide chuckles for a wider audience.

After the principal's visit, he was much easier to talk to and he seemed to take more interest in what was going on in my classroom."

Veteran teacher Faye Sturhahn agrees that communication with administrators is important.

"Dealing with administrators is probably not much different from dealing with any kind of boss, although the relationship seems to be more personal at the elementary level. I think one of the assumptions teachers make is that the administrator/principal knows what is going on in the classroom. The truth is that they don't know and won't know unless we inform them. I try to keep my principal informed about what is going on in my classroom and about the progress my students are experiencing. I have found that administrators are generally eager to hear what we and our students are doing, and by telling them, we are offering them opportunities to celebrate with us.

"Think always in terms of the other person's point of view." Dale Carnegie in How to Win Friends and Influence People

Some situations cannot be made better. If a situation is making me unhappy and affecting my teaching, then I need to make a change. I'm not afraid to ask for a new position, a new grade, or a new school. I have found that change can be very invigorating and is sometimes just the ticket I need to gain a new excitement about teaching."

Amy Billings, who has been teaching elementary school for many years, has learned she can do specific things to make her relationship with her principal more positive.

"Even though dealing with administrators may be frustrating at times, I must admit they have a very difficult job. Trying to keep the peace among children, teachers, and parents, who all have their own agendas, is not a task I would wish on my worst enemy. I have found a few strategies that have helped me when dealing with administrators.

First, I am fortunate in that the staff in our building is close-knit and a source of tremendous support. Most problems are discussed with trusted staff members before going to an administrator. Sometimes a colleague can help put things in perspective and even help solve a problem without getting the principal involved. One year when things were particularly stressful in our building, we met as a staff after school and at lunch to try to work on ways to deal with our frustrations. Our principal at the time agreed to meet with a small group of staff members on a monthly basis to discuss any problems or concerns.

Second, I have always tried to maintain a pleasant personal relationship with my principal. I think it is important for my principal to see me as a person as well as a teacher. I also try to keep that perspective about him/her. I know that he/she also has a family, goes shopping, watches movies, etc. It helps me to realize that the principal is not the be-all, end-all, authority in my life, and that he/she is only human just like me.

Finally, when the principal does something I like, I let him or her know. Verbally is good, but something written is even better. How many of us reread a positive note from a parent? A principal needs feedback too, and I think we often forget that most of what administrators hear are complaints about things they should have done something about yesterday. It is important to let them know we appreciate what they do."

Looking at issues through our administrators' perspectives will help us better understand some of their decisions. If we focus on the fact that all of us are after the same thing—the education and well-being of our children—

it will be much easier to deal with some of the frustrations we face regarding the politics of the school system.

From the administrator's perspective, Principal Gene Hill says,

"I will support my teachers as long as they can show me they warrant the support, meaning that they are acting within the policies of the district. Teachers should warrant support simply by their position, but they should not abuse or take advantage of the position. In the same manner, I expect teachers to support me. One of the things that gets us in trouble is when teachers go to the community or school board about a perceived problem or situation before talking with the principal about it. The principal needs to be involved in decisions because in the long run he or she will be asked questions about it or have to justify it. We may have disagreements, but those should be settled privately, not with other teachers within the school system or out in the community."

*"If you want something to change, do something different."
Cathy Guisewite, creator of the comic strip Cathy*

One thing that will make our lives easier is not to depend upon our principals to solve all of our problems for us. They are there as a help and a guide, but they cannot do our jobs. We want to be supported, and a good administrator will be our advocate. But if that doesn't happen, we cannot let it destroy our jobs. We must face the fact that some things are beyond our control; let go of the frustration, and do our jobs with enthusiasm.

In every relationship someone must make the final decision if there is a disparity. Teachers may be given the opportunity to offer their opinions about an issue or to come up with suggestions, but someone must actually have the final say. Between administrators and teachers, that person is the administrator. We need to accept that, trust that the administration is looking at the best interest of their faculty and students, and go on. If they are not credible, they will be held accountable for their actions. Our job is to focus on our objectives and do the best we can.

Dealing Constructively with Criticism

One unfortunate career hazard teachers face is being in a position to be judged by so many people. The list of those who consider themselves qualified to evaluate us is long: students, parents, administrators, school board members, John Q. Public, the neighbor's cat, the teacher next door. Many of these people also feel it is their right to judge how we teach, and some seem to feel it is their job to inform us or others of their opinions.

Criticism is never easy but we must learn how to use it to our advantage.

Undoubtedly, you have at some time heard something negative said about you. The way you deal with criticism is important to your state of mind. You can let it hurt you, make you angry, or cause you to want to get even. But you have other choices. You can let it go, considering the source, or you can choose to use it as constructive criticism or as a means of growth. Each of us has our own way of dealing with criticism. The best way to deal with it is our own way—the way that works most constructively for us.

The only thing that I (Beth) finally found that works for me is the saying, "What you think of me is none of my business." Before I heard this saying I was so easily hurt by even the smallest negative thing. My problem was (and still is if I don't keep it in check) that what others thought of me determined what I thought of myself. That attitude will put us on tenuous ground, because the opinions of others are as varied as the people we encounter. All that really matters is that I know who I am and what I can do. Other people have just as much a right to their opinions as I have to mine. They have a right not to like me; that doesn't change who I am. So what they think of me really is none of my business.

Lori Elliott, a teacher who is loved by students and parents alike, says,

"It's amazing that no matter how long I teach, it never ceases to hurt when I hear something negative about me. I know I'm not perfect, and I can't be everything to everybody, but I don't want to know about it. I guess I do believe that what you don't know won't hurt you. I know that I should consider the source of some of the comments, but that doesn't help. I try so hard to be a good teacher, and I love teaching and my kids so much that I can't help taking things personally. Anything you could say about me as a teacher is personal because teaching is who I am. My friends know that if they hear something that someone has said about me, not to tell me. They know I don't want to know.'

"The criticism that hurts the most is the one that echoes my own self-condemnation." Hugh Prather in *Notes to Myself*

On the other hand, I (Ginny) have a need to know when someone is critical of something I am doing. While it may be hurtful, I want to be aware of others' feelings so that I can evaluate them myself and determine in my own mind whether they are valid. It is important to me to know what others think of me. I don't expect everyone to agree with all that I do or say or to be my cheerleader, but I do value their input.

Schyrlet Cameron has learned to use criticism as a self-check.

"In life and in teaching there's going to be a lot of criticism that we can either view as a negative thing or something we can turn into a positive. I do not let criticism get me down. If I am criticized, there must be some grain of truth there, no matter how small, so I don't look at it as bad, but as positive. Instead of dwelling on it, I look at how I can grow. I say, 'Okay, this is something valid that I just don't realize about myself,' and I take that criticism and build myself up.

Many years ago (and several principals ago) I talked to a friend of mine who was on the school board about the fact that our speech teacher didn't have a door to her classroom. The speech teacher, who was new, had complained about this because her room was in a location where the noise was a real problem. My friend took up the issue at the next school board meeting, and the teacher got her a door. Sounds like a happy ending, right? Wrong. My principal came to me the following day very hot under the collar. He was angry that I had 'gone over his head' by going to the school board. From his perspective, it made him look bad and like he wasn't in control of things in his building. He told me that I had completely overstepped my bounds. I had to acknowledge that he was right. What I had done had been in complete innocence, but I had not stopped to think about the ramifications. I should have instead encouraged the young teacher to discuss the situation with him rather than taking matters into my own hands. This is an example of when a criticism against me was correct.

I have learned that it is important that I accept those things for which I am responsible and let go, or not take to heart, those criticisms that really don't belong to me. I know my strengths; I know my weaknesses; and I know to work on those weaknesses because those are where I'll get myself into trouble. I know I need to be confident about what I can do and build on those strengths. I also look at people I admire and I draw on their strengths. I may not be like them, but I can use them as a goal to improve myself."

Working with Parents

Working with parents can be a blessing or a curse, but parents are much easier to understand when we realize that our students are their children. When I (Ginny) became a parent of a school-age child myself, I suddenly began to look at my students and their parents in a different light. All parents don't parent the way we would choose. But most do care about their children and want the best for them. They do the best they can with what they know and understand. Their children are treasures to them. They are naturally partial to their offspring—and there is nothing wrong with that.

Teaching is much easier when parents are our allies.

How do we want our own children treated? I want my children to be expected to behave, so I understand that the teacher may need to be firm on occasion, but I also want my children to be treated fairly. I want to know they won't be belittled or put down. I want them to feel valued. When I understand that the parents of my students want the same things for their children, it helps me relate to them better.

Gail Emrie teaches art to junior high and high school students. She shares a trick of the trade that has helped her relationship with students and parents.

"One of the best things in the world I have learned to do is to send positive notes home. I comment on something the student has done well or report progress that has been made. There is nothing like it. The kids believe you like them and the parents believe you care about them. It seems like one of the best gifts you can give them. When some of my students did portfolios in another teacher's class, many of them included notes I had sent to them. Some of them were from years ago."

Ruth Skelton shares a different idea.

"I do think I mastered the art of communicating with parents. I learned this from a principal. She said to make the initial contact as early as you can on a positive note. Then if later you have to convey bad news, you have already established a line of communication. I followed that concept religiously. I always called my parents the first day and introduced myself. The last few years, I took a photo of each student doing some kind of work in the classroom. I bought postcards that were made for pictures and mailed them to parents. The postcards got to the house before the first week of school was up. I did the same thing later in the year, just to let parents see the progress. It was very effective."

Cheryl Stroud has learned that communication with parents is vitally important.

"I try to show that I care for and respect my students in a way they can understand. Even small things, like greeting each student at the door by name is important. One thing I try to do at the beginning of every year is to call every parent I can reach to tell them I'm their child's math teacher for the year and I'm glad for the opportunity. I also ask about special needs or abilities they can tell me about their child. This takes a couple of hours each of the first two weekends, but it's well worth it for increased communication and understanding."

Sadly, there are students from all walks of life who don't have the kind of parental involvement and support they need. In an age when it often takes all of us to make a living, parents work many hours, sometimes not leaving enough time in the day to do all they need to do for their families. We as teachers should understand—we who have trudged to school when our own children were sick, or attended a PTA meeting instead of our own child's ball game. We know it's hard. But it is also a challenge to deal with children's problems when they have no support at home.

"If you promise not to believe everything your child says happens at this school, I'll promise not to believe everything he says happens at home."
Anonymous

Susan Shivley faces this problem daily at her inner-city middle school. She says it is sometimes tough for her to feel sympathetic for the parents because she sees so clearly the pain of the children when their parents don't take time to care.

"When I was a new teacher I used to be intimidated by parents, but not anymore. I care enough about the kids to take on their parents. Before a concert I call or write parents to tell them their child will be performing for them. I am pretty bold with parents. I want them to take responsibility for their children.

Last year my students performed with the Broadway touring company's production of *Joseph and the Amazing Technicolor Dreamcoat*. The parents could buy tickets at half price. One of my students was an outstanding performer and her mother had never been to a single one of her performances.

"I don't know the key to success, but the key to failure is trying to please everybody."
Bill Cosby

She wanted so badly for her mother to come to the show and she asked me to call. My heart ached for her, so I gladly did. Her mother told me she could not come. I didn't back down. I told her that her daughter needed her to be there—that this was a big thing. I told her there weren't many seventh graders who get to be in a Broadway show. When she said she couldn't afford it, I took money out of the show choir budget to buy her a ticket. I was so glad she finally came to support her daughter and to make her feel important.

These kids face difficult situations every day of their lives. I want to give them as much love and support and attention as I can. I do care about them."

Fuel for the Fire
IDEAS TO INCORPORATE

- Stay away from negative thinkers and talkers. They can bring you down faster and easier than you can bring them up. If someone stops you in the hall to tell you the latest gossip, politely change the subject and go on your way.
- Resist the urge to talk about other people. When tempted, stop and ask yourself if it is worth your job satisfaction. Remember that talking about others can hurt you more than it can hurt anyone else. It hurts the way you feel about yourself. You do have a choice.
- Make a decision one day at a time to focus on the positive. Each time a negative thought enters your mind, trade it in for a positive one.
- Try a little experiment just for the fun of it. For one day, anytime you hear a negative comment about a person, force yourself to think of one positive thing about that person. And if you really want to feel good, make a point of finding that person and saying something like, "I thought of you today and about how encouraging you are to your students."
- Decide how you feel about criticism or gossip. If you are the kind of person who would rather not hear it, tell your colleagues not to clue you in.
- Set up a newsletter forum on your computer so you can communicate on a regular basis with parents about what is going on in your class.
- Ask for parent volunteers to talk to your class about their careers. You will be involving the parents as well as providing interesting information to your students.

Just for the Preservice Teacher

- You know what we're talking about when we talk about negative thinkers and talkers. You are in classes every day with students who complain about every assignment and every teacher. These people will be the same way when they are teachers. Now is a good time to start watching the kinds of people you "hang out" with. Look for students around you who are positive, those who get excited when they talk about teaching. Sit beside them in your classes.

- You will have classmates who irritate you or rub you the wrong way, and when you teach, you will have students who do too. When you are the teacher it will be important to find ways to get past these feelings. One way to start practicing now is to watch those people you see in your classes and look for things to like about them. Look for the positive in them, and maybe soon you will begin to like them.

Managing Our Time

How we manage each 24 hours given us reveals much about what we hold important.

If we knew how to increase the number of hours in a day, we would be millionaires. Folks in the time management business have a captive audience these days. Individuals like us, who place a higher value on our time than on our money, spend big bucks on books or gadgets that promise to help us find "more hours in our day." We buy, attend, and rely on self-help books, seminars, workshops, and planning calendars. And still we rush. Still we frustrate ourselves by committing to more than we can do.

Teachers regularly find themselves a part of this rat race. More is put upon us than we can do; or perhaps it is more accurate to say that we put more on ourselves than we can do. If your life is like ours, it's one big balancing act. What should I do first? When can I fit this in? Where did I put that? What town am I in?

A product of this overload is a stress that threatens to break our spirit and disrupt our lives. To be healthy and productive, it is necessary to find a balance. We do have a choice. Sometimes we just have to stop and say, Wait a minute. Hold everything. We may need to say no to some things. It is possible to become involved in so many things, even good things, that we're not able to do any of them well and end up neglecting the most important ones. School is an important part of our lives, but it is not our life.

Balancing Personal and Professional Life

How does life get so busy? If we could step back and look at ourselves, we would say, No wonder we struggle just to stay afloat. Teaching school, rearing a family, keeping up with the activities of the day, being involved in other organizations and clubs—we find ourselves trying to be superhuman.

You had a life before you had a classroom; nurture your personal life.

My (Ginny's) bookshelf is filled with books telling me how to organize my life, my home, my work. But none of the information in those books benefits me if I choose not to put it into practice. I have learned I do have a choice.

Ann Werland, wife, and mother of two preschoolers, says that managing her time has been a learning process.

"I have learned to use my time more wisely at school. By that I mean that I try to use the time I have effectively, not wasting it or visiting it away. I am on the block schedule with a prep period only every other day, so I have to be organized with my planning time. I try not to bring a lot of paperwork home, and I am learning to do that. But I am still having trouble with other things, such as worrying about problems the kids have. I know that things I need to do at home are just as important a part of me as things at school. I am one person at school with things to do there, and then at home I have another role. That doesn't leave a lot of time for me—the person I am. But I do try to make time for what I enjoy—for me that is reading—books, magazines, anything. Making time for myself is important."

Cathy Carleton teaches science at an alternative school. In addition to teaching, she researches and writes. She was approved for a grant that will allow her to construct an outdoor classroom to represent all the biomes of Missouri. With her guidance, her classes will grow their own wildflowers in the greenhouse and will use them to landscape the school grounds, as well as a pond and marsh area. They will also provide plants for new Habitat for Humanity homeowners. Her students will set up their own business and develop products, such as herb terrariums or the landscaping of private homes, and will learn how to keep books and do advertising. Like most of us, Cathy is a very busy lady. She says,

"I am very fortunate to have a family that understands that teaching is not an 8:00 to 3:30 job. However, I constantly remind myself not to take advantage of their understanding and tolerance. For example, recently I wanted to attend the graduation of a class from a school where I no longer teach, but whose students had worked their way into my heart. I planned to go until it dawned on me that it was the day of my wedding anniversary. I immediately changed my plans and let my husband know that being with him was more important. Unless it is mandatory that I attend some function where I teach, if there is a conflict, I will always choose to attend my son's activities.

"Money lost can be replaced, but time lost is gone forever."
Unknown

Being sensitive to what is important to my family members lets them know they are a priority. I don't get involved in many activities outside of teaching, but I do make a conscious effort to choose one organization or group in which I remain involved so I can have some outside interests and feel that I am not always dealing with 'teaching thoughts.' If you let it, teaching can dominate your life to the point of exhaustion. You must learn to pace yourself, and let some things go. Set priorities and stick to them. Remember, you must be a happy, satisfied person in order to be the best teacher you can be."

Gwen Jeffries says,

"Remember that relationships with those at home will last longer than those with anyone at work. Give the employer your best efforts for a certain number of hours a day, but always reserve time for each member of your family each day. Plan for great summers with your own children. Daydreaming about our family plans for summer has filled the minutes of a long commute and kept me going at times when my professional morale was at a low ebb."

Carla Skidmore juggles her time among the elementary, junior high, and high school bands she directs. Between band booster meetings, after-school tutoring, parades, concerts, programs, fund raisers, and her actual teaching, Carla has many school responsibilities. She also is the mother of two preschool children. How does she manage?

"I have a wonderful husband. How can I explain? My husband does not come to my concerts. I don't need him there to know he cares about me. He knows who the real Carla really is. He is supportive by arranging his schedule so he can be with our kids. He takes responsibility for them when I can't be there, and that meets the need I have. Sometimes I get very tired, but there is a difference in being burned out from teaching and being worn out. If you truly love what you do, you may get worn out, but you won't get burned out."

Cindy Nevins has a family of four children and finds herself juggling her time between work and home. She says that her husband came up with an idea that was a "big relief" for her.

"My family has one night of the school week that is reserved as my night. On Thursday nights, Billy, my husband, fixes supper or orders out pizza, takes care of the kitchen work, and taxies the kids if they need it. We don't schedule any activities on Thursdays, and the kids are to go to him if they need something. It is my night to get things taken care of for school.

Billy gave me this night several years ago because I was getting so frantic and upset at the end of each week. I have folders that I have to give back to my class on Fridays and other paperwork due, and I was finding myself doing all of the things I needed to do at home, and then staying up until one or two in the morning doing my schoolwork. This plan has worked great. On Fridays I now have time to get my lesson plans done and when I leave school to go home, the weekend belongs to the family. I don't worry about school."

Times exist when concentrating on your job actually helps you cope with problems you may be having in other areas of your life. Judy Just experienced this.

"I have learned that I cannot take my personal problems to school. There is no place for them there. School actually helps me take my mind off my problems because there I am focusing on the kids instead of myself. They remind me of my purpose. In my quest to help them, they help me. We feed and build off each other. It's a give and take kind of thing. In some ways it is like therapy. A few years ago I went through a horrible divorce. I had my first student teacher at the time, and when she left I told her about the divorce. She was shocked. She told me she had no idea that I was going through something so painful. It made me feel good that I was able to leave my problems at home and that I had not let them affect my teaching. Actually, my teaching had a positive effect on my frame of mind."

Chuck Facer has learned that it is extremely important for him to find a balance between his professional and personal life.

"Balance to me means caring for yourself as you would care for others. Walking along a nature trail, attending a theatrical production or concert, taking a day with the family (or by yourself) and doing something you want to do. Play a round of golf, find a friend and have a tennis match, take an hour to play your guitar. And above all else, cast off all guilt. It is not wrong to take time for ourselves. I find that if I do these things for myself, when I return to my daily routine it doesn't seem quite as mundane as it might have before. I have a renewed enthusiasm.

I have realized that I cannot give away something I do not have. As well meaning a teacher as I may be, my teaching is only as exciting as I am. If I am tired, depressed, or burned out, I cannot engage the attention of my students. If we as teachers close our eyes to the world around us we'll have a very difficult time opening someone else's eyes.

Ultimately, time for myself is what keeps me afloat. The joy that pervades any situation I greet with enthusiasm is guaranteed to create a higher level of enthusiasm (and joy) the next time around. It is a contagious circle, not only for me but for my students."

The Urgent Versus the Important

Charles Hummel writes in his book *The Tyranny of the Urgent* that we have become slaves to the urgent. We live in a constant tension between the urgent and the important. Exhaustion overcomes us as we attempt to attend to the many urgent things that come up in our day. Learning to distinguish between what is truly important and what is only urgent (even though others may think it is important) will help to ease this tension. Hummel says, "Hard work doesn't hurt us. We all know what it is to go full speed for long hours, totally involved in an important task. The resulting weariness is matched by a sense of achievement and joy. Not hard work, but doubt and misgiving produce anxiety as we review a month or a year and become oppressed by the pile of unfinished tasks."

The urgent is not always the most important.

This struggle can occur in all areas, including our school lives. We often find ourselves volleying among commitments. However, it's not only commitments that bring us turmoil with our time. Sometimes it's those "emergencies" to which we are summoned. There are days when we are faced with one emergency after another. Phone calls, quarrels to referee, problems to solve, disgruntled parents, paperwork deadlines, requests to aid colleagues—the list can go on and on. As much as we want to please people and to always be available, it just isn't humanly possible.

Establishing priorities for ourselves is vital to determine what will be accomplished in a day, a year, a lifetime. We can get direction from setting goals and prioritizing them, which will help us draw that line between what is the urgent and the important in our own lives. Hummel says there are four steps to help us to use our time more productively: (1) decide what's important, (2) discover how time is now being spent, (3) budget the hours, and (4) follow through.

Karen Stanley, high school business teacher, makes it a point to budget her teacher hours.

"I just decide what is important to me, what I am good at, and what I know that I am able to do. When I am approached about things that I don't really have the talents for, or that I know I won't be able to do well, I say no. I avoid being on too many committees or taking jobs just because I am offered them. I came to this decision when both of my kids were in school and involved in lots of activities. I also had my fingers in everything at school, and I finally figured out that there was no way I could do it all. I just sat myself down and decided what kinds of things I would do.

However, I'm a big one to believe that everyone should take a turn. So I do say yes to some things that aren't actually on my agenda just because I know it's my turn and it needs to be done. For example, after several years of saying no to a leadership position in our local teacher's organization, this year I agreed to be vice president, with the commitment of being president next year. After I have taken my turn, I will leave it to someone else to fill that role."

Debra Agee wears many hats. She is a family and consumer sciences teacher, as well as a volunteer with the local fire and rescue squad. She is a wife and the mother of two boys. Debra says she has done a lot of thinking about distinguishing between the urgent and the important, and she poignantly records her thoughts.

"It is 11:20 on Saturday night. I am really tired—I had a busy day. But my thoughts tonight are with two young men; one is fighting for his life in a neurointensive care unit, and the other is physically fine, but is probably struggling with the events of the day. They both made decisions that may affect the rest of their lives. The first young man apparently had been enjoying the nice weather riding an ATV, but without a helmet. It was also reported that he may have been drinking. The second young man was driving around in a car with a friend, going a little faster than the speed limit. According to the young men in the car, the ATV driver did a wheelie as he pulled out of a driveway at the crest of a hill into the highway, broadsiding the car. I am always amazed how in a split second the decisions we make affect our lives.

I respond with Pleasant Hope Fire and Rescue. Besides the satisfaction of helping people, volunteering with a rescue squad helps me keep my life in perspective. It helps me to distinguish between what I feel is important, and what I feel is urgent. It may be urgent that our rescue squad gets to an accident like the one we worked today. But it is more important that we get there! We must check our adrenaline and drive safely, even if it means stopping at a stop sign to be sure other cars are yielding to the emergency vehicle. Did you know that most fire-fighters lose their lives responding to calls?

"In truth, people can generally make time for what they choose to do; it is not really the time but the will that is lacking."   Sir John Lubbock

I think people, including myself, get caught up in the urgent and forget or fail to realize what is really important to them. I think a first step is to determine what is important to you. People need to consider that they aren't much good to anyone if they aren't healthy. The first thing we tend to give up when we get busy is time for ourselves. When teachers work themselves to a frazzle, staying up late grading papers, they aren't as productive the next day and eventually get so tired that they lose sight of what is important; they are only dwelling on the urgent. An adequate amount of sleep is important, as well as a proper diet. I also find it extremely beneficial to have time for exercise and meditation. Exercise helps eliminate stress.

We must identify the stressors in our lives and ask ourselves what is really important. We can't do everything. We have to drop the superteacher and supermom concept. My first few years of teaching, I thought it was important for me to look like the 'home economics teacher' all the time. I tried to keep my home as perfect as possible; after all, I was the home economics teacher. I felt I needed to be the best teacher and demonstrate my perfect skills in my own home. I can't say how many activities I gave up to clean house. I definitely did not want anyone over unless the house was presentable. We didn't have many people over! One day I realized the impact my attitude was having on the number of friends my children were allowed to bring over and the amount of time I wasn't enjoying with my family. I knew I felt stressed when my house wasn't at least picked up, swept, and dusted. So I finally stepped out of my Super Home Economist image and hired a housekeeper. It was a very difficult decision for me, but now I feel it was one of the best decisions I have ever made.

Because I work with the Rescue, I see some of our schoolkids at their worst. I am probably the only teacher who has seen what some of these kids are dealing with at home. It helps me better understand the students' concept of what is urgent and important. As teachers, we may feel the homework we gave is important, but if you knew what was happening in the home, you would understand the homework is only urgent. Some students are struggling on the lower end of Maslow's triangle to meet basic physical and security needs.

We have to allow our children and students to take responsibility for the consequences of their own decisions; and we have to teach them to be independent. We have to understand that everyone is different, so what a child sees as very important, we may see as inconsequential.

For myself, I have learned that I have to say no, to allow others to do things, even if they don't do them the way I would have, and to realize that the world won't come to an end if something is not done exactly the way I would want.

When I am faced with stressful choices, I ask myself a few questions. (1) Is this a life or death situation? (2) What difference or impact will this make in the future? (3) Will it be this important next week or next month? (4) Are people involved and will they be hurt? (5) What is most important to me? (6) What is going to happen if I put it off or don't do it at all?

I am not perfect. I still often take for granted those things that are truly important to me. One doesn't conquer this; it is a lifetime battle, but it is one worth fighting."

Prioritizing Your Life

Teachers will always have more to do than time will allow. One way to deal with this is to do what we need to do when we need to do it. We will always have more expected of us than we can handle. Genny Cramer, one of my (Beth's) favorite teachers, whom I've mentioned earlier, shared with me that she used to think of herself as a great procrastinator. She has since learned that what she is doing is putting her responsibilities in the order in which they need to be done. While it is true that she may not have things completed until the due date, it is not because she has been avoiding her work; it is because she has met her other deadlines first. She also says that she doesn't like to "shut the door on something" until she has to in order to keep her options open. Genny laughs and says, "I don't procrastinate, I prioritize." This seemingly simple change in perception has been an invaluable lesson for me and has relieved a lot of unnecessary stress. I, too, had thought all of my life that I was the world's worst procrastinator. Now I know I am not. I complete projects when they need to be done.

What you do today will show itself tomorrow.

Tanya Henderson still struggles with the urge to procrastinate.

"By the second week of a new school year, I find that I begin to procrastinate. I don't know if it's due to a depleted energy level, laziness, or lack of motivation, but once the newness of the year begins to dwindle, so does my productivity.

I try. I really do try. It takes great willpower to do any kind of work after the last bell at 3:10. It takes willpower to not sit on my couch and vegetate while Oprah whisks away my worries and memories of those piles of homework papers dating all the way back to a week before.

My only solution? I stay after school a little every day. I have found that when I'm at school I am more likely to get things done than when I am at home. I give myself a reasonable goal each day that I know I can reach. This has helped me deal with my tendency to procrastinate."

Others of us may not struggle with a tendency to procrastinate, but because of busy schedules we have had to learn the importance of prioritizing. As a music teacher, Chuck Facer has so many responsibilities in his job description that he has to run just to keep up. He has learned that organization is the key to helping him prioritize his obligations.

"Many of us (and I'm at the top of the list) find it difficult to organize our lives. As with many skills, however, I now know it can be learned. Funny, isn't it? We ask our students all the time to alter their thoughts and habits. Surely we can do the same! I have found a number of fine books that have assisted me in this task, among them *The Seven Habits of Highly Successful People* by Stephen Covey.

My organization strategy is to write everything down in one place that serves as the control tower of my time. Yes, I make TO DO lists with deadlines. I break large jobs into smaller ones, and I still find that organization continues to be a struggle. But I keep at it and feel a sense of real pride when a job is well done and I can cross it off my list. By writing everything down in one place I do not clutter my mind with numerous humdrum details, thus leaving room for creative thought.

"If someone throws you the ball, you don't have to catch it."
Richard Carlson

We learned in physics that life is energy. We learn in life that energy requires recharging or renewal. We learn from renewal that all things can be seen from a new perspective. When I organize, I feel a sense of accomplishment and relief at the completion of a task. Then I create time for curiosity, for learning. By being a perpetual student, I balance out my life between the adult me and the childlike me, greeting each new day with enthusiasm and wide-eyed wonder."

The endless chore of keeping up with paperwork is a pet peeve of Lee Ann Smith's, third-grade teacher. But the kids, she says, are the favorite part of her job. "There are a lot of kids who are enthusiastic and still enjoy what you do." In her search for ways to prioritize her time, she has come up with some things that have worked for her.

"I found that you could spend forever on paperwork. I have learned not to dwell on it. I have to spend time on what is important and do what has to be done. You don't have to spend all of your time on grading outside of class.

We now spend a lot more time doing things together in class. When the teacher grades everything, the responsibility is on the teacher. I think the students get more out of it when they are involved—when they grade their own papers. So rather than grading all daily assignments myself, we often check papers together in class. Before we start to grade, I assign a monitor for each group (or row). Each student has to lay her paper on her desk. The monitor glances at each paper to make sure it is the correct assignment and that it has been completed. Students without assignments then complete their work outside the room while the rest of the class is grading. They can then meet with me to go over their work during some less desirable time, like recess! Each student grades his own work. This provides immediate feedback to the child. He can see exactly what his mistakes were. Sometimes I let different students put answers on the board so the others can see the correct answer. I decided this is often more effective than grading all of the papers myself, handing them back, and having the kids pay little attention to what they missed. Obviously, it isn't a good idea to take grades on these papers, but you can always remind the students that there will be a test over similar material. Therefore, they need to grade carefully and learn from their mistakes.

I've also started using something I learned about at a gifted conference called 'most difficult first.' You introduce the concept, demonstrate how to do the work, and then do group practice. When you are ready for independent practice, you pick what you consider to be the five hardest problems on the assignment. Tell the class that anyone in the class has the opportunity to work these five problems first. If they miss one or none, that is all of the assignment they are required to do. The first person finished brings his paper to the teacher to be checked. The first person who has a perfect paper becomes the checker. The rest of the students take their papers to that person to be checked. If they miss one or none, they are free to find something else to work on. The rule is that they must work on something worthwhile that will not disturb others or call attention to themselves. If a student gets less than 80 percent correct, he or she must do the rest of the assigned page. Also any student missing one or two who does not follow the no disturbing rule must also do the rest of the page. Some students may decide they don't want to do the most difficult first and will just start on the regular assignment. That is fine. The idea is that this frees up time for kids who don't need all that drill and practice to work on things that are more beneficial to them. It is also good from the teacher's point of view, since it becomes evident who understands the concept and who may need further instruction. Instead of a student completing the assignment, but missing most of the problems, the teacher can intercede and give extra help. Another big plus is it saves a lot of grading time that can be spent in better ways such as working directly with the students. This concept can be used in any subject area where drill work is important in learning a skill."

"Saying no can be the ultimate self-care." Claudia Black

Time-Saving Tips

The problem that keeps coming back to haunt us in and out of the classroom is, where do I find time to do everything I need to do? Perhaps we are asking the wrong question; maybe we don't need to find time at all. The answer may be in saving time.

Borrowing ideas that have worked for others is admirable. It's a time-saver.

I (Ginny) have learned to "borrow" ideas from others. I heard Harry Wong, the oft-requested educator/speaker, say, "Steal anything you want from me. Everything I use, I've stolen from someone else." It's true of most of us. We see or hear of things that work for someone, and we take them and adapt them to our own situation. Most teachers agree that's a fair thing to do.

The same thing is true of managing the time in our lives. How do those around you save time in one area so they can use it in another? Everyone has learned a trick or two that has come to their rescue when it comes to making time count. In this section, we want to give you some tips that others have shared with us.

Cathy Carleton is learning how to make her life easier by staying ahead of the paperwork.

"I learned over time that it was quality, not quantity that counts. I developed many cooperative learning assignments wherein the product would be a presentation, a 'book', a program, or any number of other items. Students were given individual and daily grades for their contribution, plus a group grade for the product. These projects may last two weeks or more, and during that time I was not grading papers unless I asked students to turn in their research or a rough draft. I usually tried to schedule one of these projects in a particular class (which often encompassed two sections or more), while the other classes were doing more mainstream learning, such as reading, labs, answering questions, tests, and so on. For years, I have shied away from the 'questions at the end of the chapter' in favor of one question every two or three days, designed by me to let me know how well the students were understanding what we were learning. These are easily graded in a short period of time, and they will let you know what needs more clarification before you continue on to test review."

Veteran teacher June Brown has learned some tricks that save her valuable time.

"I have learned to (1) make a list every day and prioritize doing the most important first; (2) handle papers only once; (3) make copies of my class list to check off assignments completed, permission forms received, etc.; (4) incorporate new ideas as soon as possible; (5) file new ideas and materials as soon as I get them before they get lost; (6) respond to written mail and notes, e-mail, 'snail mail,' and voice mail as soon as possible so they don't pile up; (7) let students help with classroom chores such as watering plants, changing bulletin boards and calendars, clean-up tasks, returning and passing out papers; and (8) stay out of the teachers' lounge.

I also read time management books for new ideas that will help me in my struggle with too much to do in too little time. A particularly good one is Lakein's *How to Get Control of Your Time and Your Life.*"

More Time Savers

1. When you are giving in-depth assignments to more than one class, stagger the due dates so that you don't have all of them coming in at one time.
2. Create a system so that you don't have all skills work to grade yourself, but students are still held accountable for what they do. For example, give students credit for completing their work, and require them to make corrections on their papers, which are bound in a folder as you grade them in class. At some point during your grading period, check their folders for corrections.
3. Display an agenda for the day (or class period) on the board or on an overhead projector so that your students can see it as soon as they come in to the classroom. This will not only be a quick reference for you but it will help to improve your students' achievement as well.

4. Have a "do now" or "problem of the day" or a "warm-up" activity pre-pared and displayed for students to begin working on as soon as they enter the classroom. This will get them on task immediately, allowing your students to have more engaged time, and will save you organiza-tion time at the beginning of class.

5. Assign your students numbers according to their place in the class in alphabetical order. Always have students write their numbers on their papers. Collect student assignments by number (this could be a student's job). When you record grades, they will be in order with your grade book.

6. For elementary students, make mailboxes from storage or corrugated boxes. Label the boxes with the numbers you have assigned the stu-dents. Return papers in the boxes for students to collect at the end of the day. For an extra time saver, if your school has older students who help teachers, let them return the papers to the boxes for you.

7. If your students have the opportunity to buy afternoon milk, bring two egg cartons to class for milk count. Number each "egg hole" according to assigned student numbers. Place two containers, one with brown beans and one with white beans, next to the egg cartons. If a student wants afternoon milk, he is to put his money in the hole with his number and put a white bean in for white milk or a brown bean in for chocolate milk.

8. Allow students to mark their own lunch count. Prepare a chart with stu-dents' names and with two columns: one for bringing, one for buying. Glue Velcro patches in each spot. As students come in to class first thing in the morning, train them to immediately get a Velcro tab and stick it in the right spot for their lunch preference. Attendance can also be checked with a glance with this lunch count.

9. Delegate jobs. Students can be a big help in organizing, helping to file, tutoring, etc.

10. Use rubrics or checklists to grade writing papers or projects.

11. Taking the time to teach your students organizational skills at the beginning of the year will save you time throughout the year. Teaching them how to work in groups effectively, format their papers, and orga-nize themselves will work to both their benefit and yours.

12. Give homework quizzes. Rather than grade every homework assign-ment, have students keep their homework in notebooks and correct together in class. On specific days give a quiz over the homework. For example, number one on the quiz would be assignment #4, page 47, exercise 2, problem 3. Students would write problem 3, including the work shown and the answer. Number two on the quiz might be assign-ment #6, page 53, exercise 1, problem 7. If students have done the work and made proper corrections they will have all problems correct on their homework quiz, and you will have saved yourself much time in grading.

13. Group students at tables of four desks. Assign each person of the team a different color. Use people from the tables for tasks; for example, "Reds, pick up your table's papers and put them in the basket."

14. Instead of having all students turn in their journals (or whatever) once a week, have one table or one row turn them in each day. This way you have a few to read each day rather than all of them at once.

15. For bathroom requests, use two wooden cut-outs—one for boys and one for girls. When students need to go to the rest room, they take their cut-out, sign their name on the board, and leave. Students are allowed to use the passes only twice per day. One teacher mentioned that for sanitary reasons she has her students leave the pass on their desks rather than take it with them.

16. Prepare a substitute folder that lists your daily routine and schedule. Put in the folder materials or worksheets that could be used at any time. This saves you from last-minute rushing to prepare for a substitute teacher when an emergency arises.

As important as it is to be aware of those things that will save our time, it is just as important to recognize the things we do that waste time. How often do we finish a day thinking of the tasks left undone and kicking ourselves for wasting time? A note of clarification: Proper rest is not a time waster. I (Ginny) am guilty of feeling that I must be busy every moment to accomplish all the things I have assigned myself to do. I have had to learn to allow myself the indulgence of taking time out to do those things that we can only do in the quietness and stillness of the moment. Tucking in my children at night, sitting at their bedsides discussing the day's events, running my fingers through their hair—these are not time wasters. Reading a good book or newspaper, talking on the phone to an elderly aunt, listening to my husband's "day in review"—these are not time-wasters.

> "Why kill time when one can employ it?"   Unknown

But there are some things we do that, face it, just plain ol' eat away at our time. How about not planning ahead? Or trying to do too much at once, and not succeeding at any of it? Here's a biggie: not knowing how to say no. If we want to have an ordered life, personally, careerwise, and with our family, we must say no to certain things. Something else that cheats us of time is belly-aching over the unpleasantries that we all must do—putting the deeds off and tormenting ourselves about them rather than simply jumping in and getting them done. I've told myself, either do the job or quit worrying about it.

Another time waster is jumping headfirst into a task as if you are the only person on the planet who is capable of getting the job done. Any number of people can successfully do what you are killing yourself trying to fit into your schedule. Give others the opportunity. Lastly, worry devours time and destroys good health. It's a waste.

Fuel for the Fire
IDEAS TO INCORPORATE

- Plan a weekend getaway with your family. Include all family members in the planning.
- Spend some time daydreaming about plans for your own family. Make a list of things you have been wanting to do with them but haven't had the time. Choose a time and write it on your calendar.

- Talk with your family about the demands on your time. Ask for their support in specific ways that you can work out together.
- For a week, keep a log of how you spend your time. In your evaluation, determine how much time you are spending on "emergencies" that arise but that do nothing to help you toward meeting your goals of accomplishing the important.
- Find specific ways to help you handle stress and *do them*. Some examples are to exercise, talk with someone, make a list of things you must do and things you want to do, prioritize your list, delegate as much as you can, choose a time and place for a quiet time, follow the "one day at a time" concept, make a place for laughter in your day.
- Organize yourself: Keep a notebook/calendar with you to keep track of ideas that come to you throughout the day; schedule all activities, using a filing system for records; "declutter" your home and/or office.
- Begin your day on the right note: Establish a morning routine, get up earlier and rush less, prepare the night before.
- Determine your priorities and stick to them. Distinguish between school and home priorities.
- Plan to decline politely (just say no) invitations that do not fit into your agenda or will compete with it.
- Make a list of all the things you accomplished in the last week or the last month. Make a note of how many of those projects you completed on time. Perhaps you are not as much of a procrastinator as you thought.
- Take time for yourself. Set aside at least 30 minutes a day to read, take a walk, or do something you enjoy. Make an appointment with yourself (and call it an appointment) to do something that you have been wanting to do but have put off because you "haven't had time."

Just for the Preservice Teacher

- Make a calendar of all of your school assignments and activities to help you organize what you need to do by when. This can help relieve some of the stress of trying to remember.
- Now is a good time to make a commitment to yourself that you won't let your school responsibilities take over your entire life. Start now taking time for yourself. Go to movies, spend time during your weekends with family and friends, take time to read books and magazines for pleasure.

Collaborating with Others

One of the great things about teaching is that we are in good company—other teachers.

Working alongside good teachers is one of the joys of teaching. Our fellow teachers provide us with support, encouragement, and ideas. Teacher collaboration is important because it is often through interaction with others that teachers get new ideas and the encouragement to try new practices. Skrtic and Ware (1992) define collaboration as "problem solving through reflective discourse within a community of interests." No one can understand what we are going through as other teachers can. They help us deal with problems we encounter with students, parents, or administrators, and help us develop ideas to use in our classrooms.

Numerous educators have written on the importance of teacher collaboration. Bullough and Gitlin (1991) contend that teachers need to be a community of learners where they can support and sustain each other's growth. Newman (1990) discusses the importance of "engaging in dialogue with ourselves and other explorers." Graves and Sunstein (1992) state that "as teachers tinker and share their tinkerings with other teachers, good practice will advance." Watson and Stevenson (1989), leaders in the whole-language movement, believe that "those involved in professional change need to receive encouragement, approval, advice, and sound information about their new professional adventure." Teacher collaboration is an important component in the growth and fulfillment of teachers.

Surround Yourself with Excellence

Teaching is more rewarding when we work with people who have the same goals and dreams as we do. Teachers we interviewed spoke often of the depth of appreciation they have for their colleagues. Many stated that their teacher friends are the ones who have kept them going during discouraging times. Schyrlet Cameron told us that other teachers serve as a great source of knowledge, encouragement, and inspiration. She credits any recognition she might receive (such as when she won the Presidential Excellence in Science and Mathematics Teaching Award) to other teachers. She said she believes in "surrounding herself with excellence."

"The way to get things done is not to mind who gets the credit of doing them."
Benjamin Jowett

Kimberlea Gray says she has benefited from the knowledge of the colleagues around her. She and a fellow teacher wrote and received a district grant to travel to elementary schools with high school students who perform Shakespeare pieces.

"The best resource teachers have is each other. I do not believe teachers should be protective of their lesson plans. My teaching has grown tremendously in the last few years because of the networking in my department. I love attending conferences and learning new techniques from other teachers and then returning home to try them on my own students. This past year a colleague and I planned our honors class lesson plans together. The cliché 'two heads are better than one' really applies. We pooled our resources and, if I may say so, developed some wonderful lesson plans. We planned a Shakespearean festival together. The kids dressed up, performed skits, and participated in special activities. It was a great experience for all of us.

By working with a colleague on this, we had more ideas, an increased sense of organization and structure, and we both had someone with whom to share the enjoyment of a successful learning project for our students."

Support is Essential

Most teachers will tell you that the support they receive from their fellow teachers is one of the main ingredients in their job satisfaction. Short, Giorgis, and Pritchard (1993), who have written extensively on teacher support groups, contend that "educators need to work with each other to think, analyze, and create conditions for change within their specific circumstances that relate to their personal or professional needs." Teacher and author Routman (1991) believes teachers need to have time together to talk about what is going on in their classrooms and to "share issues and concerns and to support each other." She formed support meetings which she saw as a form of "peer coaching." She believes these meetings help to strengthen all teachers and make them all more effective.

"Success occurs in clusters and is born in generosity."
Julia Cameron in *The Artist's Way*

My (Ginny's) first years of teaching were filled with wonderful times of meeting with other young, single teachers. In the evenings or on weekends, we planned together, worked on bulletin boards, or even pulled a piano out into the hall of our school building so someone could play while the rest of us sang as we worked. Playing together was just as much a part of our lives as working together. We were in a volleyball league, which we took very seriously. We might find ourselves off for a shopping trip or to the nearby theme park for a day of fun. It was the dawn of my teaching experience, and I was surrounded with others like me. We provided one another feedback, support, and opportunities to get away from it all.

By contrast, in another teaching job I felt a great deal of loneliness. I was newly married and found myself in a town out of my home state. My husband often worked out of town, leaving me alone with my schoolwork. I remember the feeling I had when I walked into the teacher's workroom and it suddenly got quiet. Or when I would pass several teachers in the hallway and no one acknowledged me. Nothing is worse than feeling alone. It's possible to be surrounded by children or young adults all day long and still feel forsaken. I had no one in whom I felt I could confide. As I look back, it didn't take long for me to get to know some of the teachers and to feel a part of things, but I will never forget the sense of isolation, frustration, and loneliness.

Monica Andrews shares an experience she had that helped her realize the need for teachers to support one another. She took a negative situation and turned it into something good.

"The 1993–94 school year was horrible for me. I had been teaching for nine years in three different school districts. I had never had any problems establishing relationships with my fellow teachers, but for some reason I felt as though I didn't fit in at this particular school.

Looking back now, there were several reasons for this feeling of isolation. The first day of teacher inservice I wore a dress. Everyone else wore shorts or jeans. I have learned that it's always a good idea to check with other teachers before the first day to see what attire is appropriate.

Another problem was that my classroom was located in a building several yards away from the main facility. No one ever went there.

I felt even more isolated when I went to the workroom. All the other teachers had established friendships.

When my students arrived things deteriorated even more. They had loved their previous teacher and resented me for taking her place. Every day I heard how Mrs. D. did things. I was afraid to talk to anyone about the situation, fearing that I would be labeled as incompetent.

Every night I cried, dreading the next day. This went on for about three months. My husband wanted me to resign. He was trying to be supportive, but he just didn't understand. One day after school I went into a fellow teacher's room to discuss a student. I started crying, and every problem I had came pouring out. The teacher listened and then told me about others who had the same kinds of problems. I felt so much better knowing that I wasn't alone. I ended up going to her room almost every day to chat for a few minutes after school. Other teachers started coming in to talk also.

"To know the road ahead, ask those coming back."
Chinese proverb

My problems with the students were resolved after the first semester. I had to show the students that I was not their previous teacher and that I cared about them in my own way.

A few years after this, some other teachers and I decided to form a teacher support group because we saw that the new teachers who were coming in each year were having the same kinds of problems.

I think it is very important to have someone within your school system in whom to confide. It is also important to keep what is said in these conversations confidential. Teachers need to support each other as much as possible to encourage positive attitudes within the school and community."

Elementary teacher Ruth Skelton agrees.

"An understanding husband to talk over the day's problems is the most help. If not a husband, then every teacher needs a buddy to talk to. This person can usually help put things in perspective."

Flossie Parke says that most of her friends over the years have been teachers. She enjoyed doing little things at school to add some interest to the day.

"One year I suggested the teachers draw names for secret pals the week before Christmas vacation. There was much excitement around the school building as teachers slipped around to leave little surprises in teachers' mailboxes or on their desks while they were out of their room. It was as though we were small children eagerly trying to discover who our secret pals were and trying not to get caught.

"There are lots of teachers out there who are my heroes. I believe in surrounding myself with excellence."
Schyrlet Cameron, Fifth and Sixth Grade Teacher

I also liked to put a saying on my door every Monday morning. Teachers from around the building would come by to see what the saying was for the week. I enjoyed seeing their smiling faces as we began our week together.

Quite often we brought cookies or treats for the workroom. We were always on a diet, but the food disappeared almost as soon as it arrived. Little things like this made coming to school something to look forward to."

Tanya Henderson, high school English teacher, feels that caring colleagues got her through a difficult year.

"During my toughest year of teaching, I did a lot of soul-searching. Should I be a teacher? I didn't seem to be getting through to the kids! I was getting tired of daily discipline problems, conferences with parents, and most of all I was discouraged because I was trying so hard.

In my frustration I turned to my fellow teachers, who pushed me to keep going, sent me cards, and gave me inspirational books and poems to lift my spirits. They joked with me; they gave me advice; they told me about their tough years. Together we laughed and shared funny (and sometimes not so funny) stories about kids, administration, and parents. I no longer felt alone in my struggles.

During this year I also spent a lot of time writing. I wrote about my feelings and tried to make sense of them. I made lists of pros and cons. I read books about how to handle discipline. I got ideas for interesting lessons from other teachers. I worked hard and I got through that difficult year through sheer perseverance. And my teacher friends were right—the next year was better.

I hope I never have another year like that again. But if I do, I know I will keep trying. It's worth the fight."

Judy Just finds the support of teachers rewarding.

"I get ideas and learn from other teachers, but I realize I don't have to do things exactly as someone else might be doing them. I think it is important to be a team player. I like it when teachers are supportive and encouraging to each other. We work together and share our ideas and ourselves."

Laurie Whitlock has been a mentor to many young teachers during her years of teaching, but she still looks to her peers for support for herself.

"I don't know what we'd do without each other. Other teachers are my support. I think at our school we have that support from one another. If I'm having a bad day, I can go to another teacher. I can vent; I can get help. Likewise, I try to give back what has been given to me, especially when I first began teaching. I think the interrelationships of the faculty within the school are a very important part of the school. You can't be an island in your personal life, and neither can you in your professional life.

"Anytime you see a turtle up on top of a fence post, you know he had some help." Alex Haley

I am inspired by my co-workers, by what they do and who they are. I can get high on someone else's accomplishments."

Fuel for the Fire
IDEAS TO INCORPORATE

- Organize a support group for teachers in your building. Plan monthly meetings. Bring snacks and allow time for teachers to share what is on their minds. Remember to stress that confidentiality is important.
- As Flossie Parke mentioned, establish secret pals. Let teachers who choose to participate draw the name of another teacher in the building who will be their secret pal for the year or even during special times, such as before Christmas. The pal can write encouraging notes to have delivered or bring little pick-me-ups.
- Remember that some teachers cope by choosing not to participate in activities such as the ones mentioned above. These teachers need to be supported as well. Don't try to force cooperation.
- Make it a point to give an encouraging word to the people you see during the day. Especially notice those teachers who are new or seem to be having a down period in their lives. Leave little notes of encouragement in their mailboxes or on their desks.
- Share teaching ideas and strategies. Sometimes teachers need a little boost to inspire them. You can come up with more ideas together than you can alone.
- Start a teacher study group at school or with a group of your teacher friends. Teacher study groups differ from support groups in that the purpose of a study group is to learn more about an educational issue. Meet on a regular basis to share teaching ideas, accomplishments, or

struggles. Pick a topic that each of you would like to learn more about and study it. For example, you may have been wanting to incorporate more writing activities into your classroom. You can share in the reading of the literature and get ideas from one another.

▫ Write an article of teaching ideas with a group of colleagues, and send it to a journal in your subject area, such as *The English Journal, Middle School Journal, School Science and Mathematics, Instructor,* or *Mailbox.* It will rejuvenate you, and it will provide other teachers with new ideas.

▫ Like Kate Companik and a group of teachers in her school district, meet once a month and go out to eat and to a movie. Enjoy a night out with friends, relaxing and enjoying a no-pressure evening.

Just for the Preservice Teacher

▫ Organize a group of students in your teacher education program to meet once a week for lunch. Take advantage of this time to discuss class projects and assignments. Begin now working with other teachers and sharing ideas.

▫ Take the initiative to start conversations with people you sit beside in your teacher education classes. You can develop some lifelong friendships with teachers who will support you now and for years to come.

PART FOUR

BASK IN THE GLOW
CONTEMPLATE YOUR ACCOMPLISHMENTS

Knowing that we hold a key to our students' success—this is fulfillment. A teacher's tongue and actions wield much power. Words can build up or words can tear down. We become fulfilled teachers when we can see evidence that our words and deeds have lifted our students. We may never hear of the difference we made. But whether we hear or not, our joy is in seeing growth, in knowing that we tried.

A fellow teacher shared a story she has treasured for years because her mother was the one comforted by the words of a perceptive teacher. During the Great Depression, when so many had so little, children often had to "like" what otherwise would have been thrown aside in disgust. This particular little girl carried to school every day a lunch consisting of an onion sandwich. The youngsters more fortunate and less sensitive than this nine-year-old delighted in making fun of her lunch. One day the teacher of the class overheard the children's chiding. In an insightful and thoughtful moment she announced that onion sandwiches were her favorite. The little fourth-grade girl never forgot that teacher, nor has she quit telling the story of someone who lifted her up.

At times it is good to sit back and look at what we have done. After working hard to ignite the tinder and throw on the kindling, we fan the fire. It bursts into flames. It builds. It grows. Then the time is right for us to relax, just to sit back and bask in the glow. There is a time for that in teaching, too. We've worked hard, we've given it our best (not that we are ever finished), and we see signs of accomplishment. This is the time to sit back. Relax. Bask in the glow of a job well done.

When They Come Back to Thank You

A student's gratitude—icing on the cake.

As a teacher, you know the main thing that keeps most teachers ticking. Even those on the brim of burnout have the solution. It's not the paycheck or the summer "vacation" (although that helps!). It's not the enjoyment of fighting over educational philosophy or the love of grading papers. What will rejuvenate a tired teacher and hearten a discouraged one? A simple thank you will do the trick. It can be in the form of a letter, a phone call, or a "sit down and let's talk" visit. We teachers aren't picky. When a former student makes the effort to tell us that we made a difference, it goes straight to our hearts.

In our visits with teacher after teacher, we consistently heard, "I keep on because I know I made a difference in someone's life." It's worth it all when they come back to say thank you.

Finding Out You Did Make a Difference

When a student tells me (Ginny) that something I did made a lasting impression (for the good, I'm assuming), I get cold chills. I grin a little. I push the replay button so I can hear it again. We all react differently. Some teachers may tear up, while others may grab the kid and give a big bear hug. I know a few who would be beaming inside, but might just give a slight nod of acknowledgment; and then there are some who might just shuffle their feet and say, "Aw, shucks, it was nothing." Whatever the reaction, there is one thing we can count on, and that's a warm, fuzzy feeling inside. Hearing that we made a difference—there's nothing like it.

A fossil tells a story. What story does my imprint leave?

My mother has often told the story about her surprise when one of her doctors wrote a note to another doctor about her. It was especially meaningful because the one who wrote the note never knew she would see it. She had gone to an ophthalmologist for an eye problem and discovered that he was a former student. He referred her to another doctor. When she arrived for the appointment with the new doctor, he brought out a letter written to him by the former student. In this letter, he was introducing her and referred to her as "the math teacher who had taught me all I know about math." She always says she knows that she didn't teach him all he knew in math, especially since she was his junior high teacher, but it was a source of inspiration to her.

Dianne Renkoski tells about an incident that left an indelible imprint on her memory.

"I recently received a graduation invitation from one of my former fifth-grade students. She sent me a picture, and I marveled at how much she had grown. I thought to myself, 'There's my little Christine all grown up.' I hadn't seen her class since they were in fifth grade and I felt mixed emotions about attending their graduation. There was the excitement of seeing them again as young adults, but there was also the fear of thinking about how long it had been since I had taught there. Would they remember me? Would I remember everybody's name?

I went back to my class list to jog my memory about the students and their parents, and I also found a class dictionary we had made that year. Each student had written a page about themselves. They included their school picture and a picture I had taken of them. Then they wrote their names followed by a dictionary pronunciation. The first three definitions had to be descriptions about themselves; in four through six they described their personality traits; seven through ten was a list of what they wanted to do when they grew up. I laughed as I read Christine's list: '(1) I am almost the shortest person in the class, (2) my face is sort of flat, and (3) and my eyes are blue-green.' As I read these pages, I knew I had to go.

When I walked through the gymnasium doors on graduation night, the first person I saw was Christine's mom, Janette. Her eyes filled with tears when she saw me and she said, 'You don't know how much it means to me to have you here.' Naturally, she was nervous because Christine was valedictorian and would be making a speech. Janette had been very involved in her daughter's education and was always eager to volunteer the year Christine was in my room. She had been a great source of support for me, and we had become very good friends.

I was filled with pride to see my former little fifth graders walking in proudly in their caps and gowns. I recognized every one of them even though they were taller and more grown up. Then the Salutatorian, Angela, got up to make her speech. She began by thanking her mom and dad and family for the influence they had had on her life, and then she said, 'I would also like to thank my fifth-grade teacher Mrs. Renkoski . . .' I was so shocked I can't even remember everything she said. And then it was Christine's turn. She also thanked her family in her speech, and then much to my surprise she said, 'And a special thanks to Mrs. Renkoski for teaching me that learning can be fun and for helping me realize my potential for life.' I sat there with tears rolling down my cheeks and a lump in my throat, and I thought, This is why I teach. This is what it's all about. I became a teacher because I wanted to make a difference in some kid's life, and there stood two of my students from seven years before telling a gymnasium full of people that I had made a difference in their lives.' I was overwhelmed. No one knew I would be attending the graduation ceremony, and later I discovered that neither girl knew the other was going to mention me in her speech.

"I think you will find that great, historic feats are rare, but the joy of life is made up of obscure and seemingly mundane victories that give us our own small satisfactions, our own personal pleasures, and our own momentary revelations."

Billy Joel

You always have those bad days when you sit and throw your head on your desk and say, 'Why am I here?' Then an experience like this makes those days all worthwhile. I know why I teach."

One thing that keeps Vera Ker going is seeing a struggling student succeed in life. In watching him or her succeed, she knows she has made a difference.

"I didn't start out to teach special education. It was not until I began substituting that I found real satisfaction in helping the child who was trying so hard to learn. It sparked me to be creative in the ways I could teach subject matter. With that spark I returned to college to become certified in special education. Teaching students with special needs is what keeps me coming back every day, every week, and every year to help those students gain the knowledge they need to graduate.

I remember one student who first came to me in the seventh grade. After working with him for several years, I began talking to him about vocational school and about getting into electronics. That boy received a four-year scholarship in electronics, graduated with his degree, and now works for a leading electrical firm.

I know I made a difference because of my perseverance and steady pressure for him to follow the rules, complete his assignments, and to come to the resource room for help. I made phone calls to parents, was a friend who would loan lunch money or listen to a problem about his girlfriend, parent, or another teacher.

To witness the success of a student who was doomed for failure is one of the unpublished, hidden benefits that comes with being a teacher."

Gay Lynn Russell, a high school counselor, faced the challenge of changing school systems recently. She says,

"After you've been somewhere for a while, you don't have to establish rapport every year. When you begin a new job or start in a different system, it takes a good part of the year to establish rapport and develop trust. When that happens, it makes you feel good. Every time someone gets a job, is admitted to a college, gets a scholarship, especially if they couldn't go otherwise, it makes you feel good. Every time someone who drops out of school decides to come back for all the right reasons, it makes you feel good."

It's Not the Pay But The Payoff

The payoff comes from the appreciation of our students. We all know we didn't become teachers to get rich. But we find we become quite wealthy in terms of the love, fulfillment, and friendships we acquire. One word of thanks can carry us for days. Teaching is a profession in which we don't receive many accolades. Other teachers offer support, and administrators will occasionally boast about the group of teachers as a whole, but often the only thanks we get is a word here and there from our students or former students. But that's enough. We just need to hear every once in a while that someone has appreciated the time we have invested.

The rewards of teaching are often private and heartfelt.

Mary Wright has found that she still runs into students she had years before and is thrilled when they tell her they remember.

"Would I choose to teach again? OH YES! The look in the eyes of a child when learning takes place is a joy far up on the top of my list of great happenings. I get such a thrill when years after a student has left my classroom, we meet in a store or on the street. I remember encountering one such student.

'Aren't you Mrs. Wright, and didn't you teach math at Pershing Junior High School?' I was suddenly transported back to the classroom where a red-headed 'overly-active' child is performing an unforgettable vocal demonstration of his unwillingness to 'show his work' on a math assignment. His whole world was aware of his unhappiness at what he considered unnecessary work.

'I didn't like you,' he says, jarring me back into the present, 'or the way you taught. You were hard on us.' (No surprise to me; I wasn't running a popularity contest. I was trying to teach so learning would take place.) And then, he continues, 'I had hoped I could see you again to thank you for not only teaching math skills but also teaching organization and study skills. You made college much easier for me.'

What I heard was a dream come true. You often wonder if all that struggle had been worthwhile, and here, maybe just once, you know it has been."

Our pay may not be as great as that of other professionals, but as Judy Just explains,

"Teachers may not get much respect these days, and sometimes we even get bad press, but we have to know within ourselves that what we do, or don't do, makes a difference in this world. And even though we may not get big bucks, we educate the doctors, lawyers, and business people. We have to know that what we do, what we stand for, and what we are makes a difference. Sometimes when we forget, we have to remind ourselves and each other. We can't let the negative tear away at us.

I get a big payoff from being a teacher. Even after 27 years I still enjoy decorating my room in August; I still enjoy trying something new; I still enjoy working up a new unit or theme; I still enjoy getting new materials to use; and most of all, I still enjoy the kids."

Ann Werland feels the payoff comes when her former students are able to use the skills they learned in her class.

"I remember one girl I had in Spanish. She was a challenge, but there was something about her that I really liked. Since school didn't really matter to her, I had to have patience as I helped her learn how to get through the day and find what she needed to make things work. It seemed I was working with her more on those things than Spanish. When I saw her a while back, she had lots to tell me. She had just gotten married and she said, 'I want to thank you.

We went to Cancun on our honeymoon, and we got into a taxi. The driver was talking on and on in Spanish, and I answered him! I talked to him!' She said her husband asked her how she knew that, and her reply was, 'Mrs. Werland's Spanish class.' She told me she had graduated from school. I was excited to find that my sticking it out with her had paid off."

Although, Gwen Jeffries began her career as a Spanish and social studies teacher, she now finds herself as a high school librarian. She feels rewarded when students remember her.

"Proverbs 31:28 describes a good woman. It says her children will rise up and call her blessed. The same is true of a good teacher. Not all students return to give effusive thanks, but former students do have a way of turning up at the nicest times. One of my students repaid me by being an absolutely outstanding first-grade teacher for my own two children.

Nine years after I taught the one-and-only social studies class I ever taught, I went to the hospital to deliver our son. I chose to have anesthesia. As I groggily became conscious, I saw a beautiful red-haired nurse above me saying, 'Do you remember when we . . .' Can you believe she still remembered what we had done in social studies class? Suddenly it was all right that years before an older, more staid teacher from across the hall had come to the door of my classroom because we were laughing too loudly as we planned the project. We all had fun. We all remembered what we did and why we did it."

Thank You Can Be More than Words

I (Beth) spent my first year as a teacher pregnant with my first son, Joe, who was born the following summer. On the last day of school I received a big surprise. My students and their mothers had a baby shower for me. I walked into the gym and there sat my mother and mother-in-law, along with most of my students' mothers. There was a table piled high with gifts, including a hand-quilted baby blanket, toys, diapers, and everything I would ever need for a new baby. I'll never forget sitting at that table surrounded by my students who were begging, "Please open mine next." I love those kids and I will never forget how much they meant to me. I will never forget the kindness of their parents. What a wonderful way to begin my teaching career.

Teachers receive thanks from parents and students in ways other than words.

Cathy Carleton talks about how glad she is when students look her up just to see her.

"I don't remember having students return and thank me for being their teacher, but I've never felt slighted by that. Many students have gone quite a bit out of their way to visit with me and let me know how they're doing. I even had two young men track me down at another school so they could invite me to their graduation. Whenever I run into students at the store or the mall, they always smile and stop to visit. I'm always glad to see them. It's a joy to know they've turned out so well. That's thanks enough."

Norene Fields, an English teacher nearing retirement learned a lesson in her first year of teaching that has inspired her throughout her career.

"On my first day as a new teacher I was given some 'inside information' from another teacher. She took me aside and told me about three brothers I needed to watch out for. She said they were losers and nothing but trouble, and she thought I should be aware of it. I knew she meant well and was trying to help me as a new teacher, but I also realized those were things that should have been left unsaid. I was determined to accept the challenge of working with those boys.

As the year went on, one of the brothers spent a lot of time in my room. He would come in to talk with me while I was working at my desk. I still remember him squatting down to be at eye level with me.

Years later, I was shopping at the mall, and I ran into his wife, who recognized me and got my attention. We visited for a few minutes, and then I went on my way. After a while, a young man approached me and introduced himself as the boy I'd had in class. He said he had walked all over the mall looking for me. He said, 'You sure were a tough teacher, but you were fair. I just want you to know that I turned out okay. I'm not setting the world on fire, but I'm doing all right. I am a good citizen involved in my community; I have a decent job and make a good living for my family.'

"Everything one does as an individual affects the whole."
Serge Kahili King

It was a good feeling to know that he had sought me out to let me know about himself. I'm glad he knew that I would care. Those rewards are what teaching is all about."

Cheryl Stroud finds joy in seeing her students succeed. She remembers one very special moment.

"My greatest accomplishment and thrill was probably discovering two nonreaders in a large class and finding ways to teach them math. Since they couldn't read they thought that meant they couldn't learn math either. I happened onto one of those two students about six years ago. He glowed as he told me of his business—that does very well—and for which he does most of the accounting!"

Lori Elliott has found that seeing the proud looks in the faces of the parents of her students is rewarding.

"Every time I see one of my former mothers she reminds me of the time when her son sang a solo in our cowboy program. She talks about how it just melted her heart to see her little boy standing with his cowboy hat held to his chest while he sang 'Home on the Range.' She said that the year when her son was in my fourth-grade class was their family's best year because he was so happy and loved coming to school. So what keeps me going is not only seeing the children succeed but also seeing the look of pride in the eyes of their parents. You live for these moments—the moments when you know you've touched a child, thereby impacting their parents as well."

Judy Just shares a favorite memory.

"Having taught so many years in one school, I see many former students as adults with children of their own. Several years ago I had one of the orneriest little boys I have ever had. I dearly loved this boy, but he gave me a run for my money. I hadn't seen him in years when one night he came to a PTA meeting to see his child perform. When I walked in, he saw me, came over, gave me a big hug, and introduced me to his wife. I felt all kinds of warm fuzzies in his simple act of kindness.

Another time I had a little boy who nobody liked much. He had a terrible temper and had to go to another place for a while. I felt close to him and saw a sweetness not many others could see. He went through some tough times. Years later I was sitting at my desk after school when a tall man came into my room. I looked up and saw the boy, now a man, come toward me with outstretched arms. After a good hug, we had a nice long conversation. A few days later he brought me a gift that will always be very special to me."

Cindy Wilson has taught many grade levels. Now as a college teacher who helps prepare preservice teachers, she feels that seeing her students pass on what she has taught them is reward enough.

"Daily, little things keep the light burning for me, such as seeing the enthusiasm of a student as he or she accomplishes a task. It is knowing that interest triggers more learning, having colleagues try something I do with their students, showing me something they do to help me build a stronger foundation for my teaching.

It is also those lifetime moments like when former students return and share how wonderful their lives are and that my teaching impacted them, when parents send me thank you notes saying I made a difference, when students or colleagues recommend me to others, or when I just sleep soundly at night knowing I did a good job."

Letters of Appreciation

When the teachers we interviewed were asked, "Why are you teaching? What keeps you going?" they would often reach into a drawer or filing cabinet and pull out a box, envelope, or folder. "It's these," they would respond. Though they may have different names, they all contained the same ingredients: letters of appreciation.

Kimberlea Gray thought back on her own   *Just a little note to say . . .*
student days, remembering a teacher who made a
difference in her own life. She wrote him a letter of appreciation, and here for us she shares her feelings about the importance of saying thank you.

"You never know how you touch someone's life. Eight years after graduating from Republic High School in Republic, Missouri, I decided to write to my former agriculture instructor, Mr. Vencil Mount. I had written a paper for a graduate class describing the teacher who had made the greatest impression on my life and career, and I wanted to share it with him. I told him about my personal and professional life, but most of all, I wanted to thank him for believing in me and encouraging me throughout high school. Though I never entered an agriculture-related field after high school, I felt that the every-day skills and values that Mr. Mount instilled in me carried on to my classroom. He nurtured a love of public speaking, a talent that has been invaluable throughout life. Mr. Mount encouraged me even though he knew I would never directly use my agricultural knowledge; thus I try to believe in my students even though they may not write a great novel.

Mr. Mount wrote back and thanked me for my praise. Several months later when I saw him at a local car wash, I approached him and introduced myself. He politely shook my hand but appeared confused. I added that I had written a letter to him sometime earlier. His eyes began to sparkle and he raised his eyebrows in excitement. He gave me a huge bear hug and then rushed me to the other side of his car to see his wife. The look in Mr. Mount's eyes at that moment made me so happy that I had written and thanked him for his dedication to education.

Since that time, I have wondered how many of us take the time to write that special person who made a difference in our lives. I know that my thank-you letter meant a great deal to Mr. Mount, but I also know that it meant a great deal to me. When my one-year-old daughter begins school in four years, I want to instill in her the practice of thanking her teachers for their hard work—for their sake and hers.'

"Here is why I teach," Dianne Renkoski said as she handed over a let-ter she had received from the mother of one of her students.

"Thank you for all the time you have spent with our daughter and the other children in the class. I have seen so many changes in these kids. They have grown up so much this year and it's because of their teacher. You have put a lot of love and understanding into these kids and they need that as much as they need the learning.

Thank you for being a great teacher to our daughter and to all the other chil-dren in the class. Words can't express the true meaning of what a teacher really is. They have to be loving, understanding, caring, yet hard so the children can learn. This is what I look for in a teacher, and what I found in you. Thank you once again for letting our daughter have that chance in your class."

Gay Lynn Russell has collected what she affectionately calls her "Smile File." In it she has many cards, letters, and notes from former students and parents who want to let her know what she has meant in their lives. A rewarding part of her job is helping students get scholarships for college. One former student wrote,

"Since I despise writing, it was Mrs. Russell's determination which got me through the application process. She gave me guidance and encouragement. And I thank her every semester when I have no school bills to pay."

Gail Emrie has a file of thank you's. She pulls it from a drawer and gently opens it. The contents are varied, but one of the things in it is a picture taken at a school prom. Gail and a young man are standing together, both with broad smiles. On the back is a note to her from the boy. "I'm fortunate to have known you. You taught me a lot and for that I thank you."

In the file are cards, letters, notes. Included is a letter in which the following was written about her:

"I have been inspired by her desire to travel to new places and to learn from her experiences. She shares moments of her life with the class. She helped me decide on my career as a graphic artist and, even though she isn't aware of it, she has given me the confidence to believe I can make my dreams come true."

Fuel for the Fire
IDEAS TO INCORPORATE

- Keep a notebook on your desk and make a practice of jotting down those little comments students say that make you know they enjoy having you as a teacher.
- Keep a special file in your desk in which you can quickly throw in little notes from students or their parents. On days when you are feeling discouraged, you can pull out your file and read the comments to help you remember why you are there.
- Write a story about a time when a student told you that you had made a difference in his or her life. Put it in a special place where you can treasure it. We often think we'll never forget what a student has said, but over the years the memory can grow dim.

- ☐ Make a list of all the things you like about teaching. What are the pay-offs for you? And, yes, it's okay to mention June, July, and August—even though those months get eaten away with planning and schoolwork.
- ☐ Make a list of pros and cons about teaching. Which weighs heaviest for you? It is our bet that the rewards outweigh the negative. If they don't for you, perhaps it's time to make a change either in how you teach, where you teach, or even if you should still teach.
- ☐ Think back to all the times former students have come by just to say hello.
- ☐ Don't be discouraged if you don't hear "thank you" verbalized often. There are many other ways to know that you have made a difference.

Just for the Preservice Teacher

- ☐ It won't be long until you have cards, letters, and little presents from students who have taken the time to tell you how much you have influenced them. You may already have some from your field experiences in the schools. Start collecting them now by buying yourself a special notebook or box to keep them in. These little treasures are joys to look at and cherish.
- ☐ Elementary teachers probably get more notes and mementos from students than teachers of older students, but that by no means indicates that they are more appreciated. Those college teachers who have supported and encouraged you would appreciate a word or note of thanks as well. Take a moment to tell them "thank you" or send them a card. Let them know when you get your first teaching job. They will want to share in your excitement.

Enjoy Yourself

It's time to relax and enjoy being a teacher.

A time may come in our stressful, busy lives when we need to sit down and take a good look at the life we have created for ourselves. We have worked hard to establish a positive learning environment in our classrooms. We strive daily to make learning meaningful for our students. We have meshed our teaching philosophies with our teaching styles and our personalities. We have created classrooms that are communities of learners in which we, too, are learning. Perhaps now we can relax and do what we came here to do— enjoy being teachers.

My family (Beth's) has a tradition each Christmas, as many families do, to watch the movie classic *It's a Wonderful Life*. It serves as a reminder to us of how lucky we are to be alive and to have one another. One of my favorite parts is when George Bailey "wakes up" from his vision of what the world would be like if he had never been born; he is running through the streets shouting, "Hello, Bedford Falls," "Hello, you wonderful old Building and Loan." Things in his life that used to be sources of disappointment and sorrow had become sources of joy and reward. It was all in his perspective. We can change our perceptions much as George did by looking at what "might have been" in our own world. Next time you walk through the halls of your building and into your classroom, think about George Bailey. Can you say, "Hello, you dusty old chalkboard" or "Hello, you crowded room"? Try looking at what is around you and imagine what your world would be like without your impact.

At the end of each semester, while of course I'm thrilled for a break, I am also just a little sad that it's over. It's not school I will miss so much, but as the song says, "We'll never pass this way again." Some students I will run into here and there, and some I may never see again. My mom tells me that when we were kids and visiting our cousins, the same thing would always happen. She would come tell us it was time to leave for home, and we would all cry out in unison, "But we just started having fun." For me, the same applies to teaching. Just when you finally really get to know one another and things are really clicking, the term is over. I guess that's a good way to end a semester. And it's a good reminder to me to enjoy every moment I have with my students. A reminder to enjoy being a teacher.

Elementary teacher Cindy Miller is an example of one who enjoys her job. She says,

"I love going to school. I get a chill that runs up and down my spine every day because I'm that enthusiastic about the lesson plans I have prepared. I know I am going to have great days because I expect great days. I know if I keep my attitude positive and expect the best, I will get the best. A positive attitude has a lot to do with how your day will end, even before it begins.

I stay positive about my job and avoid burnout by remembering all of the things that my students have accomplished—not only how they have made better grades but how they have grown as people. Sometimes teachers forget that we teach our morals and values by example. Our students learn as much from us when we are not teaching. In the morning when they get off the bus and talk to me about the football game on television the night before or the fishing trip they took, I use these opportunities to show them I care about them. Sometimes the stu-

"Be happy with what you have and you will have plenty to be happy about."   Irish proverb

dents share personal triumphs or failures. In return I give them my undivided attention and a part of my heart. This keeps me inspired to teach.

When I start to get discouraged I stop and think back to how badly I want-ed to be a teacher. I dreamed about making my room a comfortable, enjoyable place where students would enjoy learning. My students rely on me to set a positive, happy atmosphere for the classroom every day. That is part of my job description.

When my students come to school it is their home away from home. I try my best to make them feel comfortable by being friendly, patient, and understanding. In return, the students allow me to share in the joy and excitement of understanding something for the first time. How could a per-son not be overwhelmed with happiness when one of his or her students has finally mastered a difficult problem? I hold on to these joys and record them in a journal and remember why I am there. Remembering the light of under-standing that comes on in their eyes renews my spirit about teaching. I love being a teacher."

One of the reasons Lori Elliott loves being a teacher is because she can make her job anything she wants it to be.

"I want to enjoy school and I want my students to enjoy it, too. Yes, I do entertain them because I want them to want to come to school. And I entertain them because I enjoy entertaining them. I like to make them laugh. It's part of the fun of teaching for me. I do it because I want to and because they enjoy it.

If I am introducing a unit on cowboys, I may very likely show up for school that day in a cowboy outfit complete with hat and holster. I will have cowboy music playing in the background as I tell them the story of the char-acter I am portraying. My room will be decorated to the hilt with cowboy paraphernalia, and lesson plans will have been developed that provide hands-on activities for every subject area.

And I will be having a ball. I live for this stuff. I like to cut loose and have a good time with my students. School is a fun place for all of us."

Leslie McIlquham has learned to revel in the positive atmosphere cre-ated by children, which she has coined "childspace."

"I love laughter—not that loud, boisterous noise emanating from the lips only—but, laughter bubbling up from the deepest part of our being—the laughter that bears evidence of the sheer delight of becoming. Childspace filled with the sweet sounds of laughter, giggles, cheerfulness, gladness, happiness, pleasure, and delight is the place I love to be.

It is here in childspace we can feel the almost tangible power of joy. It is here we are reminded of who we are. Here in childspace we gain understanding of the simplicity of successful living. Here we celebrate the journey, that great adventure we call life."

Portrait of a Fulfilled Teacher

When we talked with Esther King, she said something that was a little hard to believe. But we knew her. And we knew it was true. She said that she doesn't ever get up in the morning and not want to go to school. Isn't that unbelievable? She loves being there—*always*. Now that's not to say that she doesn't get a little frustrated with things that go on sometimes. Nor does it mean that the pain that often plagues her doesn't interrupt her enthusiasm now and then. But when it gets right down to it, she wants to teach. She wants to be with her first graders, and she wants to listen to them read. She usually feels better once she is there, she insists. And we believe her.

"Happy teachers makes happy kids." Lori Paro, veteran elementary art teacher.

Esther King has taught first graders for the last 24 years of her 31 years in elementary classrooms. As one parent wrote about her when she was selected by the Southwest District Missouri State Teachers Association as Educator of the Year in 1992, "Now the people in the southwest area are going to know what people in Aurora have known for years."

Esther has a reputation—and a scrapbook of cards, notes, and letters to prove it—of being a teacher who cares and one who gets results. But it's not just the students who are motivated in her classroom. Esther herself is motivated. She thrives on watching her students' progress.

"Seeing how children blossom motivates me. Learning to read makes them feel good about themselves. I'm always excited to hear the children read, to see their progress, and every morning my helper and I listen to each individual child read."

Students notice and appreciate her efforts, as is evidenced by many notes from her first graders. *"You are kind. You are a wodrfle teacher. You are so nice I want to be in your class next year." "Thanks for teaching me to read." "Mrs. King is beautiful like a butterfly."*

Former students also come back to say thank you. One, Susan Hunter, describes her thoughts about Mrs. King, the teacher she says she most respects.

"Mrs. King did magic in that little basement classroom. She was, and is, the teacher everyone wanted, and I truly believe she made a tremendous impact on my life. Mrs. King is a tall, graceful woman with a soothing voice that she never raises; she does not have to because students hang on her every word. Oftentimes her voice is barely above a whisper, as if she is telling a secret that every child is waiting on the edge of his seat to hear. Her thoughts are positive and encouraging, and she is always smiling. The lessons she teaches go beyond the classroom. She does not simply teach students to read, but gives them a love and excitement of literature by showing all that it has to offer. Saying 'I'm sorry' is as important as saying your ABC's, and laughing is just as important as being quiet. Study time was strictly adhered to, but so was running and playing at recess.

"Gratitude is the memory of the heart."
                    Jean Baptiste Massieu

Mrs. King did not just teach me how to learn; she taught me to love to learn. Every day was an adventure, every lesson a new and exciting challenge. She challenged those students who were constantly pushing ahead while nurturing those who were staying behind. She had a calmness in her eyes that encouraged you to do your best for her; no one wanted to let her down. And when you succeeded at even the smallest task, the praise was endless.

Mrs. King always found the best in students and taught them to see the best in others. She was concerned with more than basic classroom lessons and affairs; she wanted children to be happy and successful in every aspect of their lives. She somehow gave every child a bright future and a beautiful heart. She worked miracles in her room by showing us the miracles the world had to offer.

Mrs. King's concern extends beyond her first-grade classroom. She remains in touch with students, keeps a journal of cherished student work, and is proud of every accomplishment a former student makes."

Parents also find themselves returning to Mrs. King to thank her for who she is and what she has done for their children. Below is a sampling of parent comments in notes and cards:

- "He learned so many things from you—you are a beautiful example for children."
- "What I admire most is the fact that you have made some progressive moves for the children's benefit. Most people who have been as successful as you have for all those years would have refused to change."
- "Thanks for being such a good role model for our children."
- "Thanks for making a difference in the lives of so many young people and their families—including ours."
- "Since I've had a daughter in your room I am really qualified to say that the reason your reputation is so good is because you are good. I have really seen growth in Amy this year in academics, confidence, and maturity. You have been instrumental in her growth."
- "You are so special to our family! Stephanie has learned so much this year; we have a hard time believing it's only been three months ago that you became a part of our family! Thank you for the book you gave to Stephanie!"

- "I wanted to formally thank you for taking an interest in Bob this year and not only teaching him 'the academics' but providing an atmosphere where many of the true lessons of life exist and can be learned. I truly admire your positive attitude and the Christian traits you have demonstrated to these children."

- "Words cannot express my appreciation to you for making Teara's first grade so fun and enjoyable. You are truly a remarkable teacher."

- "Mere words cannot express a parent's gratitude for the lessons you've taught and the guidance you've given one's child. You have been a blessing in our lives, as DJ has made considerable progress this year. Moreover, she has really enjoyed her first-grade year, which is so important!"

- "Mrs. King, keep doing what you're doing! It seems to be working!!"(included with a copy of a former student's high school grade card showing all A's)

- "I was a volunteer mother in Mrs. King's class. As a parent, those were probably the most beneficial years of my parenting. Mrs. King was teaching me and dozens of other parents how to love, nurture, and discipline our children. She did this by her example. Even today, not a week goes by that I don't think to myself "How would Mrs. King handle this?" In [her] classroom each child is made to feel loved and valued. Praise is abundant, but always honest. Somehow Mrs. King turns the classroom into a family and support system for each child. Honesty is of utmost importance. Mrs. King's first graders know right from wrong. There is no moral equivocation in her class. Yet she is never judgmental and always affirming. I saw children from the most underprivileged backgrounds begin to grow and blossom in her classroom. Perhaps even more importantly the other children learned to be kind and find value in each and every classmate. There are no "losers" in Mrs. King's room. I never heard Mrs. King raise her voice or make a negative comment to a student. When a child leaves Mrs. King's first grade he knows he is a person of worth."

What is her secret to success?

"I keep two inscriptions on my desk as daily reminders that how I treat each child will greatly affect his self-worth: 'I am what I think you think I am,' and 'The misbehaving child is the discouraged child. Give him constant encouragement.' I think you have to get on the child's level and make him feel worthy. I think that is the big thing—to make the child feel accepted. Far too often, children are labeled and categorized. These external judgments frequently become self-fulfilling prophecies. I believe that making a child feel worthy by encouraging the 'I can' attitude is one of the most important gifts a teacher can give.

"There are two ways of spreading light; to be the candle or the mirror that reflects it." Edith Wharton

I have had the privilege of watching the self-esteem of my children soar as they have mastered the fundamental skills of reading. By communicating to my students the wonderful world that is opened to them after they learn to read, I have witnessed the joy they experience when the printed word comes to life. Learning to read does not guarantee success, but illiteracy makes failure virtually inevitable."

Esther wants to get off to a good start with each of her children, even before the school year begins. So throughout the summer, she arms herself with a paperback book, a broad smile and lots of encouraging words, and off she goes to enter her children's worlds. She says that she is sold on visiting in her children's homes because she can learn so much about the children through the visits.

"I visited one little girl from a very poor family. Her mother said it would be the girl's second time in first grade. The little girl said, 'I can't read. I don't know the words.' I answered, 'That's what we're going to do in first grade. If you knew all those things you wouldn't come to first grade. I don't even know everything.' After we'd visited awhile, she looked up at me and said, 'I want to go to school now.'

Another time I visited in a little boy's home. His mom said, 'You're going to have your hands full with him.' She even said it to him, too. The home visit helped because I recognized that he had some needs that I could compensate for. I could see that he received mostly negative feedback at home. When he walked into my classroom on the first day, I welcomed him. 'I'm so glad you're in my class this year.' He ended up being one of the best students in my class. He was a little frisky, but he was a great student, and he wasn't hard to handle."

Esther expects a lot from her children. But she allows them to be children. She knows they need to move about, and she takes advantage of that. Part of her secret to success is found in knowing her children and using their childlikeness for their own benefit.

"I have found that integrating movement with memorization produces results almost like magic. In memorizing the vowels, I lead my children in cheers. We all stand and wave first the right arm, then the left, as we yell: 'A,E, I, O, U!' Then everyone jumps as high as possible and yells: 'The vowels!' After a few cheers, all the children have learned the vowels. While learning to count by fives, we hit our thighs with both hands on fives and clap hands on zeroes. I have had children with limited skills master counting by fives in one sitting. In my classes we march around the room, wave arms, jump, hop, or whatever best captivates the children's attention for the task at hand. No child daydreams during these activities!"

As is obvious from the number of appreciative notes she receives from parents, Esther makes it a point to involve parents in the school lives of their children. She gives them a calendar to sign when their child reads to them and says this is a very big deal for the children.

"Ideally, they should read to their parents every day, seven days a week. Each month, all of the children who have their calendars signed on each day are invited to a dinner party in our classroom during lunchtime. We darken the room, light candles, play classical music—they love the classical music. The children love it, and their parents work hard to get the calendars signed. I've even had parents come by school on the way to or from work to tell me they forgot to sign the calendar that day. This is a real treat for the kids and they work extremely hard to be able to come to the monthly dinner party.

Another thing we involve the parents in is a Mother's Day tea party. I plan a program and each child has a speaking part. After the program, the children get their mothers, seat them at their desks, and serve them cookies and punch. I do all of these things because I believe that children succeed more when their parents are involved."

Why is Esther King like the Energizer bunny—going and going and going? She says she's not quite sure herself.

"I just like to go to school. I like all parts of it—seeing the students come in to the classroom every morning. They always want to tell me something when they come in, and I look forward to listening to them. I look forward to hearing them read. There is always improvement. I have a friend who says 'practice makes better,' and I really believe that. If you look for it, you can see progress in every area—academically, in their behavior, in showing kindness, helping others.

"If you have knowledge, let others light their candles at it." Fuller

I deal a lot with character. I tell my children, 'What you are when no one is looking is what you really are.' I can begin by saying, 'Character is . . .' and the children can finish it for me. I talk a lot about self-discipline, telling them that it's the only kind that matters."

Esther King is an example of a teacher who succeeds. She succeeds in the classroom with her students' learning. She succeeds in her communication with parents. She succeeds in sharing a part of herself with her students and in helping them to see what it means to be a productive, caring citizen. But she is successfully meeting her own needs as well. She loves what she does. She thrives where she is. She is fulfilling her passion for making a difference. She is one who has kept the light in her eyes.

Fuel for the Fire
IDEAS TO INCORPORATE

☐ Set this book down and close your eyes. Think of what the world would be like if you had never been born. Be specific. Contemplate individual students' lives you have touched. What might their lives have been like if you had not been a teacher? What would your school look like if you weren't there?

☐ Make a list of things you can do to become more fulfilled in your teaching career. Pick one that you can do today. Do it.

☐ If someone were to draw a portrait of you as a teacher as we did of Esther King, what would it look like? Are you a fulfilled teacher? Make a list of what it would take for you to be fulfilled. Work on one thing at a time to make your job into the kind of job you want it to be.

Just for the Preservice Teacher:

☐ Make a list of what you think it takes to be a fulfilled, happy teacher. Hide that list away somewhere to read when you are teaching. Or frame it to remind you of what kind of teacher you want to be.

☐ Interview someone you know who is still happy to be a teacher. Ask specific questions about what it is that keeps him or her fulfilled. Write down the answers and keep them in your teaching file. As a special gift for that person, write up your interview and give it to the teacher.

SPREADING THE LIGHT

This book was written for you, by two who are just like you. Some of you may live in a state of constant contentment, but most of us find ourselves teetering between being captivated by our jobs and being disheartened.

In our combined experience of nearly 30 years in the classroom, we have seen many teachers come and go. Some of them needed to go. They weren't meant to teach; they didn't have the heart for it, or the patience, or the knowledge, or the talent, or something. They just didn't belong in the classroom. But many of them left teaching because they were tired and frustrated. They had lost the spark. They needed some encouragement or support and hadn't found it. The truth is, we all paddle that same boat at times. One teacher we interviewed said,

"There have been times when the thought to change careers weighed heavily on my mind; then out of the blue, a present or former student or parent came by, and as they talked and shared, they said things that, unbeknownst to them, lifted and encouraged me. I praise God for these times, and I stay a teacher."

The profile we have given of a fulfilled teacher is a portrait of an actual person. But she is not the mold into which every teacher must force himself to fit. We hope that through this book, we have encouraged you in your differences. Each of us has our own personality, method, and style. Just because we don't do something the same way our favorite teacher was able to do it doesn't mean we aren't good teachers.

We all feel failure at times. We all feel frustration. We all feel anger. That's normal. What makes us that teacher with the light in our eyes is that we know how to get up and go again.

Many teachers from all over the country have contributed to this book. Everyday, ordinary teachers like ourselves. We were inspired as we heard from such a variety of people the same basic story: "Teaching has meaning to me." We found something very interesting as we talked with these teachers. Though they were a sampling of professionals—friends, colleagues, family, acquaintances, friends of friends—it was almost as if we had hand-picked people from a teachers' hall of fame. Each person in his or her own way had something extraordinary to say, something profound, something of significance. There were award winners, grant writers, creative geniuses; and there were teachers who tenaciously persisted in giving their best. As one teacher said, *"You catch the spirit of teaching, the spirit of learning, and the spirit of caring; they all go together."*

In this book are stories from hundreds of cumulative years of hard experience—the best kind of schooling. These ordinary teachers were doing fantastic, exciting, meaningful things in their classrooms. We have looked to our own; they are fountains of wisdom.

"Teachers are the true heroes of the world."
Unknown

REFERENCES

Ayers, W. (1990). Rethinking the profession of teaching: A progressive option. *Action in Teacher Education, 12*, 1–5.

Bullough, R., & Gitlin, A. (1991). Toward educative communities: Teacher education and the development of the reflective practitioner. In B. R. Tabachnick & K. Zeichner (Eds.), *Issues and practices in inquiry-oriented teacher education* (pp. 35–55). London: Falmer Press.

Byrne, B. M. (1992, April). *Investigating casual links to burnout for elementary, intermediate, and secondary teachers.* Paper presented at the Annual Meeting of the American Educational Research Association, San Francisco, California.

Cooper, J. M. (1994). The teacher as a decision maker. In J. M. Cooper (Ed.), *Classroom teaching skills.* Boston: D.C. Heath and Company.

Garrett, S., Sadker, M., & Sadker, D. (1994). Interpersonal communication skills. In J. M. Cooper (Ed.), *Classroom teaching skills.* D. C. Heath and Company.

Graves, D., & Sunstein, B. S. (1992). *Portfolio portraits.* Portsmouth, NH: Heinemann.

Heath-Camp, B., & Camp, W. G. (1990). What new teachers need to succeed. *Vocational Education Journal, 65*, 22–24.

Hollingsworth, P. M. (1990). Reading teacher burnout and stress. *Reading Improvement, 27*, 196–199.

Martens, M. L. (1992). Inhibitors to implementing a problem-solving approach to teaching elementary science: Case study of a teacher in change. *School Science and Mathematics, 92*, 150–156.

Newman, J. M. (Ed.) (1990). *Finding our own way.* Portsmouth, NH: Heinemann.

Perrone, V. (1991). *A letter to teachers: Reflections on schooling and the art of teaching.* San Francisco: Jossey-Bass.

Reutzel, D. R., & Cooter, R. B. Jr. (1992). *Teaching children to read: From basals to books.* New York: Macmillan.

Routman, R. (1991). *Invitations: Changing as Teachers and Learners K–12.* Portsmouth, NH. Heinemann.

Sadker, M., & Sadker, D. (1994, February). Why schools must tell girls: "You're smart, you can do it." *USA Weekend*, pp. 4–6.

Short, K. G., Giorgis, C., & Pritchard, T. G. (1993, April). *Principal study groups and teacher study groups: An interactive and innovative approach to curriculum change.* Paper presented at the Annual Meeting of the American Educational Research Association, Atlanta, GA.

Skrtic, T. M., & Ware, L. P. (1992). Reflective teaching and the problem of school organization. In E. W. Ross, J. W. Cornett, & G. McCutcheon (Eds.), *Teacher personal theorizing: Connecting curriculum practice, theory, and research* (pp. 207–208). Albany, NY: State University of New York Press.

Watson, D. J., & Stevenson, M. T. (1989). Teacher support groups: Why and how. In G. S. Pinnell & M. L. Matlin (Eds.), *Teachers and research: Language learning in the classroom* (pp. 118–129). Newark, DE: International Reading Association.

INDEX